TELL ME THE ANSWER

BOOK 3

by
Indira Mukherjee

bluebird books

BLUEBIRD BOOKS
An imprint of Sachdeva Publications
Jaina Complex, 2-B, N. S. Marg
Daryaganj, New Delhi-110002
Tel. : 3277655, 3287586
Fax : 91-11-3276876

ISBN : 81-7582-002-0

First Published in Dec. 1997

Printed by
Shivam Printers, Delhi

Illustrated by
Keshaw Art Studio
Delhi

Typeset by
Microtech Computer Communications
Delhi

Rs. 110.00

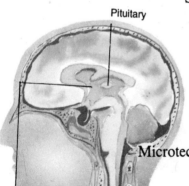

Pituitary

Hypophysial Veins

Contents

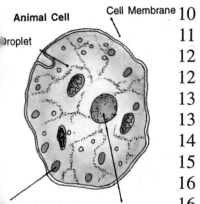

The World We Live in

Animal Cell

Cell Membrane

Droplet

Storage Granule

Nucleus

How Things Began?

Electrons

Nucleus

Carbon Atom

How Things Are Made?

Human Body

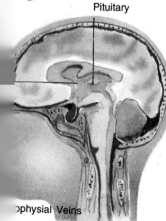

Pituitary

physial Veins

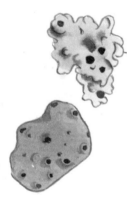

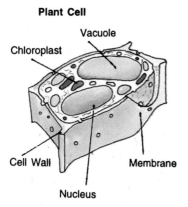

Plant Cell

Vacuole

Chloroplast

Cell Wall

Membrane

Nucleus

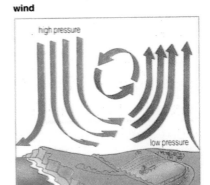

wind

high pressure

low pressure

What makes a Wind?

Can the scientists make Protoplasm?

The World We Live In

How does the Weather man forecast?

How fast does the Earth move ?

Sanjeev asked - "We know that the earth has two motions. It spins around on its axis and it moves in an orbit around the sun. Ma'am, how fast does our earth move ?"

Ma'am replied - "Let us first know how fast does the earth rotate about its axis. The period of rotation through 360 degrees (One complete turn of the earth) takes 23 hours, 56 minutes and 4.091 seconds. It is this rotation which causes the changes of day and night.

When the earth moves around the sun, it is closer to the sun at some points in its orbit than at other points. The point of orbit nearest to the sun is called "perihelion" "while the point of orbit farthest from the sun is "aphelion". The earth and all planets move in their orbit at a speed that depends on their distance from the sun. A planet moves faster when it is closer to the sun than when it is farther away. So it moves fastest at perihelion and slowest at aphelion.

At perihelion, the earth moves in its orbit at a speed of 30.2 kilometres per second. And at aphelion, it travels at the rate of 29.2 kilometres per second."

How does the Weather-man forecast ?

Sweta asked - "How does the weather-man forecast ?

Ma'am replied - "In order to understand this we have to know what is weather. Weather is a condition of the air or the atmosphere at a particular place at any given time. No matter what the air is- cold, cool, warm, hot, calm, breezy, windy, dry, moist or wet — that's weather. Weather changes from hour to hour, day to day, season to season and even from year to year.

The weather forecasters observe these

changes very carefully They know that the daily changes in weather are caused by storms and fair weather moving

over the earth. They know that the seasonal changes are due to the turning of the earth around the sun. The most important "cause" of weather is the heating and cooling of the air. Heat causes the wind. As well as the different ways in which water vapour appears in the atmosphere.

One of the ways the weather forecaster studies the weather is to look at the "fronts" that exist. Fronts are boundary lines between the cold air moving southwards from the north and the warm air moving from the tropics. Most of the severe storms which cause rain, snow and other types of weather are in some way related to these fronts. The weather forecaster when finds low pressure, he/she knows that storm is likely to occur because cold air is moving in to replace warm rising air that is laden with moisture. High pressure indicates fair weather.

The weather forecaster forecasts on the basis of certain facts about weather and on the basis of the reports of the weather in most parts of the country."

How is Humidity measured ?

Rabiya asked - "Ma'am, what is humidity and how is it measured ?"

Ma'am replied - "The word humidity simply means the presence of water vapour in the air. It is found everywhere, even over great deserts. Due to water in atmosphere, we have clouds, fog, rain, snow and warm, sticky days.
The instrument which is used to measure the amount of water vapour in the air is a hygrometer. The most accurate kind is called the wet and dry bulb hygrometer. Two thermometers are mounted side by side on a base. The bulb of one is covered with muslin or some coarse material which is kept wet. The bulb of the other is left bare and dry.

If the air contains much water vapour, the moisture on the wet bulb evaporates slowly and the wet bulb thermometer does not show much lowering in temperature. If the air is dry, the moisture on the wet bulb evaporates rapidly and the wet bulb thermometer shows a much lower temperature than the dry bulb thermometer. There are other types of hygrometers that use currents of air or chemicals or a hair to measure the increase or loss of moisture in the air."

What is Water ?

Ravinder asked - "Ma'am, water makes up a large proportion of all living things. And it is a tasteless, odourless, colourless thing, what is it ?"

Ma'am replied - "It is a tasteless, colourless, odourless compound which is present everywhere in the soil and exists in the air. What is it made of ? It is a simple compound of two gases hydrogen, a very light gas ; and oxygen, a heavier active gas. When hydrogen is burned in oxygen, water is formed. But water does not resemble either of the elements which compose it. It has a set of properties of its own.

Water, as it occurs in nature is never pure in the true sense. It contains dissolved mineral material, dissolved gases and living organisms.

It exists in three states, like most other matters; a liquid state, a solid state called "ice" and a gas called "water vapour". At 0 degrees centigrade or 32 degrees fahrenheit, water changes from the liquid to the solid state or freezes. At 100 degrees centigrade or 212 degrees fahrenheit, it changes from the liquid to the gaseous state. Without water, life is absolutely impossible. Life doesn't exist in other planets because there seems to be no water there."

What is Matter ?

Namrata asked - "Ma'am, water is called matter and then this chair is also matter! What is matter ?

Ma'am replied - "Matter is anything that takes up room anywhere in this universe. Chair and water, both take up room, don't they ? So we can say matter may be a liquid or a solid or a gas.

We have divided matter into two types: "organic" and "inorganic". Things that are living are "organic". For instance- human beings, trees, flowers, animals. But then, cotton and woollen cloth are also called "organic". Why? This is because they were once part of something alive.

And "inorganic matter" are those things that are not living or that were never alive. For instance iron, glass, tin, water.

All matter is built of "atom". If all the atoms were exactly alike, there would have been only one kind of matter in this world. But there are more than 100 kinds of atoms.

When matter is made up of only one kind of atom, it is called "element". Iron, Iodine, Gold, Oxygen are elements. And matter that is made up of more than one kind of atom joined together is called a "compound". A group of atoms is called a molecule. When atom and molecules are packed together more closely in matter it becomes dense. And matter that has great density is also heavy like Iron. Why is wood lighter ? It is because wood is less dense.

Can matter be ever destroyed ? No, never. It can be changed from one state to another and can be changed into energy, but it can never be destroyed."

How small is a Molecule ?

Ranvir asked - "Ma'am, a molecule is the smallest particle of a matter, isn't it ? How small is a molecule ?"

Ma'am replied - "No, molecule is not the smallest particle of a matter - Molecules differ greatly in size. For example, a molecule of water is made up of two atoms of hydrogen and one of oxygen. But the molecule of pure natural rubber has about 75,000 carbon atoms and about 120,000 hydrogen atoms!

Simple molecules like that of water are only a few billionths of an inch in length. The rubber molecule is thousands of times larger.

It is really impossible for us to imagine how small molecules are. For example, let us take 10 cubic centimetres of air. In this space there are over 300 million billion molecules. And that bit of air is not packed tightly because it actually has a great deal of empty space!

Did you know some molecules are shaped like footballs while others are long and threadlike ?"

Can the scientists make Protoplasm ?

Mekhla asked - "Ma'am, all organisms, whether they are plants or animals, are composed of cells. And the cells enclose protoplasm which is the main life substance. Can the scientists make protoplasm in the laboratories ?"

Ma'am replied - "No, I'm afraid not. The scientists, so far, have not been able to make protoplasm, the living part of all plants and animals.

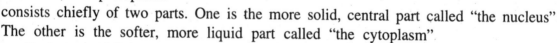

It may be a whale, a rose, a human being—the walls of the cells enclose the same life substance called protoplasm. In each cell, the protoplasm consists chiefly of two parts. One is the more solid, central part called "the nucleus" The other is the softer, more liquid part called "the cytoplasm".

Each type of living thing has its own kind of protoplasm. So all protoplasm is not alike. And the different types of cells within an organism have special forms of protoplasm.

Though protoplasm varies, 99 percent of its bulk is made of carbon, hydrogen, oxygen and nitrogen with traces of many other elements. Protoplasm also stores and releases all the energy that plants and animals have. What makes protoplasm alive is still unknown! You may grow up to be a scientist and may solve the mystery."

Can Cellulose be produced in the laboratory ?

Shaoli asked - "Ma'am, can cellulose be produced chemically in the laboratory ?"

Ma'am replied - "No, I'm afraid, it can not be. You know that cellulose makes up the softer parts of the bodies of plants. And it is the cellulose which enables a plant to bend and have flexibility.

We can't produce it in the laboratory. Nearly all green plants manufacture cellulose for their own use. It is made up of the same chemical elements as is sugar, namely, carbon, hydrogen, oxygen.

Though we can't produce it, we do use it in many ways. Raw cotton is one of the purest forms of cellulose found in nature and the cotton fibres are used for making cloth. In making of paper, cellulose is being used. By treating cellulose chemically in various ways, many things can be produced. For instance, the base for photographic films, threads such as rayon for weaving, cellophane and various other plastics.

If we eat cellulose, we won't be able to digest it. Goats, camels who have certain bacteria in their stomachs are able to digest cellulose with the help of these bacteria."

What is Chlorophyll ?

Simon asked - "Ma'am, what is chlorophyll ?"

Ma'am replied - "It is chlorophyll due to which the plants are green. It is the green colouring matter in plants. And it is this chlorophyll which enables the plants to take

substances from the soil and the air and to manufacture food. Human beings and animals are also dependent on it because without it no plants could have existed. Even those creatures which live on meat depend on other creatures who live on plants. We can trace any food back to its original source and find it was made by a plant.

Chlorophyll is contained in the cells of leaves and often in the stem and flowers. With its help, the plant's living tissue is able to absorb the energy from sunlight and to use this energy to transform inorganic chemical into organic or "life giving" chemicals. This process is called "photosynthesis". The word comes from the Greek words which mean "light" and "put together".

You must be wondering about plants which have no green colour to help them in making their own food. Mushrooms and a whole group of fungi have no chlorophyll. How do they get their food ? They get their food from other plants or animals or from the decaying remains of plants and animals.

Chlorophyll is extracted from plants and is being used by us in many ways, including destroying certain bacteria with it."

What are Fungi ?

Nimish asked - "What are fungi ? Some people say it's important to us, while others say it's dangerous!"

Ma'am replied - "While some fungi do a great deal of good, some other fungi do a great deal of damage. They help us by causing decay so that rubbish doesn't accumulate endlessly. This also returns mineral salts to the earth which plants need. There are even fungi which create drugs and which are used by us to fight disease. But there are other fungi which cause diseases of plants and animals and we have to fight against them.

Fungi are simple dependent plants. Why are they called "simple" plants ? Its because they don't have roots, stems and leaves as complex plants have. They are dependent because they have no chlorophyll which means they can't manufacture sugar from

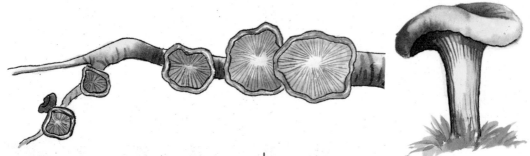

carbon-dioxide and water as green plants do. They depend on food that has been made by green plants.

There are a great many different kinds of fungi, and they differ in their structure. Some fungi consist of a single cell. For example bacteria and yeasts. The average length of bacteria is about 0.005 millimetres. The big group of fungi called "moulds" range from those that live on bread to those that attack damp fabrics. Certain moulds give flavour to cheese and others are used to prepare drugs. Mushrooms are also fungi.

What are Protozoa ?

Neha asked - "Ma'am, what are protozoa ? Are they animals ?

Ma'am replied - "Yes, they are. They

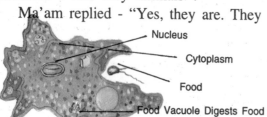

Nucleus

Cytoplasm

Food

Food Vacuole Digests Food

are the simplest animals known to exist since they consist of a single cell. If you

could examine a teaspoonful water from a pond under a microscope, you would be surprised to see more than a million tiny animals swarming about in the water. These are protozoa.

You will notice that protozoa live in water or in moist places. Although they are made up of only one cell, that cell can carry on all the tasks necessary to keep an animal alive. It can hunt and eat food, digest it and make it into living matter. It can breathe and burn the food it eats and throw off waste. It can also reproduce itself.

How do they reproduce ? They reproduce themselves either by dividing themselves into halves, each of which becomes a complete, separate animal or by growing little swellings, called "buds" which break off and form separate, new animals.

There are some protozoa which have tiny shells of chalk with little holes and when they die, their shells fall to the bottom and in the course of centuries, their skeletons create chalk deposits. Some protozoa cause malaria and sleeping sickness.

There are more than 15,000 different types of protozoa."

When did Plants appear on Earth ?

Debabrata asked - "Ma'am, when did plants appear on earth ?"

Ma'am replied - "The land was bare and lifeless when life first began on earth more than two billion years ago. The only plant life was in the sea.

Then, about 425,000,000 years ago a few small green plants appeared on land. They may have developed from certain kinds of green sea weeds. The first land plants looked very much like the mosses,

liverworts and hornworts you see growing in damp and shady places.

More complicated plants existed about 400,000,000 years ago. These resembled modern ferns, horsetails and club mosses. Ferns were the first plants to have roots, stems and leaves.

By the time the first dinosaur walked the earth, vast forests of seed ferns, ginkgoes, cycads and cordaitales stretched across the land. These were the first trees to reproduce by seeds.

Pines and other conifers (cone-bearing trees) developed somewhat later, 300,000,000 years ago. This group includes many familiar trees such as pines, firs , spruces, cedars, hemlocks and redwoods. All these trees bear their seeds on cones.

About 150,000,000 years ago, the first flowering plants developed. Their well-protected seeds gave them a great advantage over plants with more exposed seeds, and they increased in numbers and kinds. Today these flowering plants are found everywhere."

What in the Soil makes plants grow ?

Nishi asked - "What in the soil makes plants grow ?

Ma'am replied - "Actually there are many things in the soil that make the plants grow.

Let's first know what exactly is the soil . Soil is a mixture of organic and inorganic materials. The organic part is the living things and the remains of once-living things. And the inorganic part is made up of non living things like rocks and minerals.

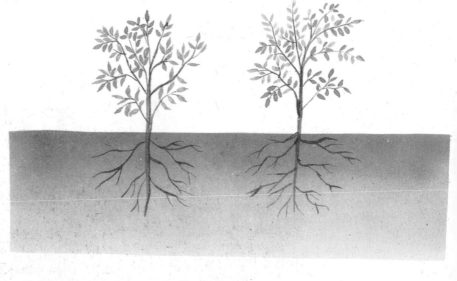

Humus is the decaying organic matter in the soil. This humus separates otherwise tightly packed rock particles, thus allowing more water and air to enter the soil. Humus also provides food for bacteria and other micro-organisms in soil. Plants can use the dead organic matter. Humus is good for the fertility of the soil.

There are many kinds of animals living in the soil. The body wastes of these animals enrich the soil. Earthworms turn over the soil and improve it. Micro-organisms feed on particles of organic matter. This breaks the organic material into minerals, gases and liquids. These are good for plants.

Moreover there are ten elements that all plants need to grow. Three of these, oxygen, hydrogen and carbon, are present in either air or water or in both. The others are obtained from the soil by the plants. They are : nitrogen, phosphorus, potassium, calcium, magnesium, iron and sulfur. All these help the plants grow."

Was the soil once rock ?

Amrit asked - "Ma'am, I read somewhere that nearly all the soil that exists in the world today was once rock. Is it true, ma'am ?"

Ma'am replied - "Yes, it is. And then, for millions of years together, nature has been at work, weathering and crumbling the rock into the tiny fragments we call soil.

How is it done ? This is done in many

ways. Heat and cold cracks off surfaces of rock. Wind blown sand wears away rock. Glaciers scrape rock surfaces. Running water carrying mud and sand rubs away rock surfaces. Waves beating against a shore pound rocks into smaller and smaller pieces. Certain bacteria give off acids which help crumble rocks.

According to the size and quantity of the rock particles in it, soil has been classified. Sandy soil is composed chiefly of sand. Clay soil has very fine particles and tends to be heavy, cold and damp. "Loam" is a kind of medium mixture of sand and clay. Stony soil contains a large proportion of rocks or pebbles. "Muck", or peat soil, has few rock particles and is made up chiefly of decayed vegetation. The soil in which plants grow is a complex substance which also contains mineral salts, decayed organic matter and living organisms."

How are Fossils formed ?

Anupama asked - "Ma'am, how are fossils formed ?"

Ma'am replied - "A fossil is actually the remains of plants and animals preserved in rock. When a plant or animal dies, it gradually disappears. The soft parts decay. The hard parts are worn away by wind and rain. But if it is covered by sand or other substances, parts of it remains preserved for a long time and turn into fossils.

Sometimes an entire animal is preserved. Or a fossil can be a film of carbon left by a decaying plant. It might be the track of animals walking across mud. Most fossils are remains of plants and animals that lived and died in water. Their bodies became quickly covered by sand carried in the water. Gradually more sand and mud covered the bodies, pressing down on the layers of sand underneath. The bottom layers hardened into rock, a form of rock called "sedimentary rock".

On land, the bodies of plants and animals may be covered by blowing sand or by ashes from a volcano. Insects and

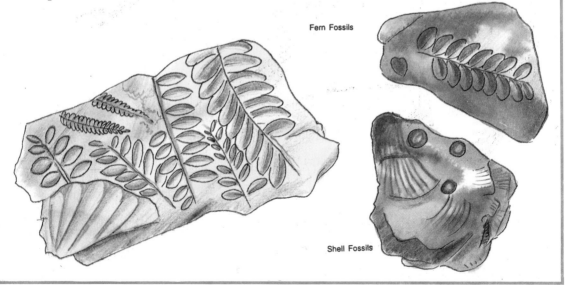

Fern Fossils

Shell Fossils

17

other small animals may be trapped in sticky sap. If this sap hardens into amber, it preserves the bodies of the animals inside. Larger animals may fall into tar pits or quicksand and their bodies may be preserved for millions of years."

What are Vertebrates ?

Ruchira asked - "Ma'am, what are vertebrates ?"

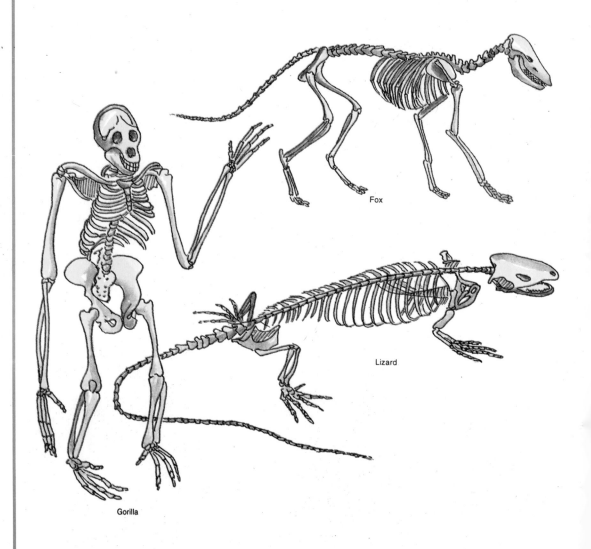

Fox

Lizard

Gorilla

Ma'am replied - "Vertebrates are those who have a backbone or vertebral column. We have one thing in common with birds, snakes, fish, cows, frogs and that is the backbone or vertebral column.

The vertebral column is made up of many small pieces of bone called "vertebrae." So we are called vertebrates. You will notice that snails, crabs, sponges, grasshoppers do not have a backbone. So they are called "invertebrates".

At one end of their backbone, the true vertebrates also have a bony,boxlike structure which contains the brain. Their nerves run together into large bundles which are carried in a cavity in the backbone to the brain. The nerves make contact with every part of the body in a vertebrate.

Vertebrates also have fine, hair-like blood vessels which carry food to every cell in the body. And they combine to form large arteries and veins which run the length of the body to the heart.

Vertebrates never have more than four limbs. In fish, the two pairs of paired fins correspond to the limbs. In birds, one pair of limbs has developed into wings. In us, one pair is arms, the other, legs."

What is Dust ?

Rahul said - "Ma'am, its so amazing that dust from the desert region of the Sahara has been noted to fall in London!

Ma'am - "Yes, that's really amazing! Dust consists of tiny particles of solid matter that can be carried away in suspension by air. Dust is usually lifted by the wind from one place and is carried along by air currents until it finally settles because of gravity or it comes down with rain.

Dust is produced by a wide range of conditions. It may come from soil that is being blown about, from the exhaust of heavy traffic, from the burning of fuel in homes and industry and from volcanic activity, forest fires and ocean spray. Ocean spray produces about 2,000,000,000 tonnes of salt dust in the air every year.

"Dust storms" take place in areas where drought has removed natural vegetation. Such storms put thousands of tonnes of dust into the air and this dust may end up somewhere as far as 2,000 miles away !"

What is Quicksand ?

Sriya asked - "Ma'am, what is quicksand ? It is very dangerous, isn't it ?"

Ma'am replied - "Quicksand is actually not dangerous if you know what it is and how to deal with it. It is a light loose sand which is mixed with water. It does not look different from sand which might be right next to it. But of course there is a difference : quicksand does not support heavy objects. People who step into quicksand do not sink out of sight. Since it contains water, they would float. And as quicksand is heavier than water, people can float higher in it than they do in water.

You will find quicksand usually near the mouths of large rivers and on flat shores where there is a layer of stiff clay under it. Water is collected in the sand because the underlying clay keeps the water from draining away. This water may come from many different places such as river currents or pools.

The grains of quicksand are different from ordinary grains of sand because they are round instead of being angular or sharp. The water gets between the grains and separates and lifts them so that objects tend to flow over one another. This makes them unable to support solid objects. Some quicksand is not even made of sand. It can be any kind of loose soil, a mixture of sand and mud or a kind of pebbly mud.

One has to move slowly in quicksand if one steps into it. This is to give it time to flow around the body. Once one does this, it will act like water in which one is swimming."

Are Deserts always hot ?

Rohan asked - "Ma'am are deserts always hot ?"

Ma'am replied - "Let's see what is the definition of a desert. A desert is a region where only special forms of life can exist because there is a shortage of moisture. Now, when we go by this definition, the Arctic is really a desert ! There is less than 40 centimetres of rainfall a year and most of the water is frozen. So it is properly called a desert. It means deserts are not always hot. The great Gobi desert in the middle of Asia is bitterly cold in winter times.

Most of the dry, hot deserts are found in two belts around the world, just north and south of the Equator. They are caused by high atmospheric pressures that exist in those areas and prevent rain from falling.

Other deserts, which are found farther away from the Equator are the result of being in the "rain shadow". This is the name for an effect that is caused by mountain barriers that catch rainfall on their seaward side and leave the interior region dry.

A river may rise in moist areas and cross great deserts on its way to the sea. The Nile flows through the desert region of the Sahara and the Colorado River flows through a desert too. But no great rivers originate in deserts."

How do Clouds stay up in the sky ?

Diya asked - "Ma'am, how do clouds stay up in the sky ?"
Ma'am replied - "It is the air currents which keeps the clouds up in the sky. A cloud is a collection of moisture in the air. When the cooling continues, more and more water vapour is changed into drops. And gradually these tiny droplets become larger and larger as they collect more moisture. When the drops become so large that they can no longer be held up by the air currents, they fall to the ground as rain. Thus the air currents can hold up the cloud as long as the drops are small.

At many different heights above the earth, clouds can form. In fact clouds are divided into types according to their distance from the earth. The four main families of clouds are high clouds, middle clouds, low clouds and clouds which may extend through all levels."

How does Light travel ?

Sumit asked - "Ma'am, how does light travel ?

Ma'am replied - "When you drop a pebble into a pool, it makes waves, does'nt it ? In the similar way lighted particles start pulses or waves.

You know light is a form of energy. And like other forms of energy heat, radio waves, and x-rays, the speed, frequency and length of its waves can be measured.

Its behaviour in other ways makes it similar to these other forms of energy too.

Did you know the speed of light ? It travels at about 186,000 miles per second. This means that in a year, a beam of light travels 5,880,000,000,000 miles ! That is the distance which astronomers call a "light year" and it is the unit used to measure distances in outer space.

Actually, one of the great mysteries of the world in which we live is light. We still do not know exactly what it is. We can only describe it in terms of what it does."

How fast does Sound travel ?

Akrit asked - "How fast does sound travel ?"

Ma'am replied - "The sound travels in various mediums like air, water, objects, even the earth. Ancient Indians used to put their ears to the ground to hear a distant noise. The speed of sound depends on the medium.

The speed of sound in air is about 335 metres per second (750 miles per hour). But this is when the temperature is 0 degrees centigrade. As the temperature rises, the speed of sound rises.

Sound travels much faster in water than in air. When water is at a temperature of 8 degrees centigrade, sound travels through it at about 1,435 metres per second or 3,210 miles per hour. And in steel, sound travels at about 5,000 metres per second or 11,160 miles per hour.

It is not the pitch which affects the speed of sound but it is the medium. For instance, if you clap two hands together once under water, and then outside water, you'll be amazed how much better sound travels through water than through air."

What is a Cyclone ?

Robert asked - "Ma'am, what is a cyclone ?"

Ma'am replied - "A cyclone is a kind of storm and a storm is simply air that is moving rapidly from one place to another.

A storm starts when warm, moist air from the Equator moves northwards into the Northern Hemisphere and meets a mass of cold dry air moving southwards from the Arctic region. These two kinds of air

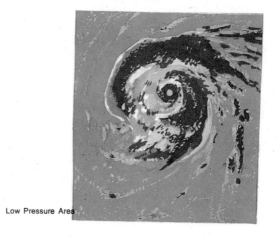
Low Pressure Area

masses do not mix. The sharp boundary that is formed where they meet is called a "front". As the air masses continue to move, the lighter, warm air climbs up over the cold air. As it is forced upwards, the warm, moist air is cooled. The moisture then condenses, forming clouds.

While all this is going on, the air pressure begins to fall at the centre of the storm. The winds begin to blow around the low pressure area in an anti-clockwise direction. Thus the warm, moist air moves northwards around the eastern side of the storm, while the cold air moves southwards around the western side.

A low pressure area is know as a "cyclone". The mass of air in such an area could vary in diameter from 400 to 1,000 miles."

What is a Tornado ?

Ayesha asked - "Ma'am, what is a tornado ?"

Ma'am replied - "A tornado is simply a special kind of cyclone. It is also a circular storm and is confused with a cyclone. But while a cyclone is 400 to 1,000 miles in diameter, a tornado may be only 30 to 1,600 metres in diameter.

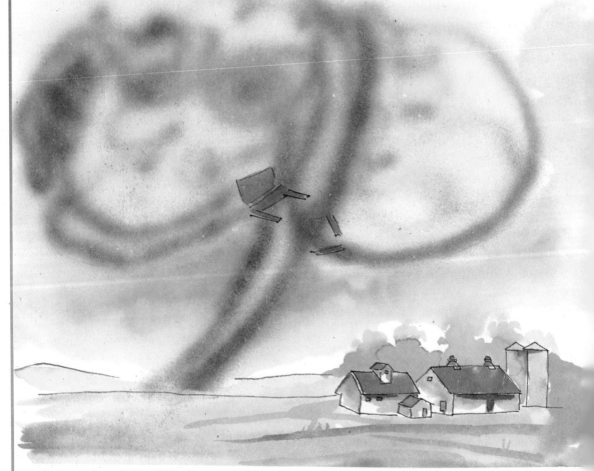

A tornado arises when the conditions that cause ordinary thunderstorms are unusually violent. There is an updraft of air. There are winds blowing in opposite directions around this rising air. This starts a whirling effect that is narrow and very violent. When this happens, centrifugal force throws the air away from the centre. And this leaves a core of low pressure at the centre.

This low-pressure core acts like a powerful vacuum on everything it passes. This is very destructive. It can actually suck the walls of a house outwards in such a way that the house will collapse. The other destructive thing is the high winds that may blow around the edges of a whirl. These winds can reach 300 miles per hour and nothing is safe against them".

What is Hurricane ?

Rohit asked - "Ma'am, what is a hurricane ?"

Ma'am replied - "Hurricanes are storms that start in the tropics. In a hurricane, the storm area is usually from 100 to 400 miles in diameter and winds around the hurricane may reach speeds of 75 to 125 miles per hour. A special feature of the hurricane is the calm, central part of the storm which is called the "eye" of the strom. This eye is about 5 to 15 miles in diameter. As it moves over an area, the winds become almost calm. This sometimes leads people to believe that the storm is over. However after the eye passes, the winds begin to blow with equal violence from the opposite direction. Since a hurricane is a circular storm, the winds move in a kind of circle as the storm itself moves.

Hurricanes strike the USA mainly in Gulf of Mexico area and also all along the eastern coast. When exactly the same kind of storm takes place in the East Indies and the China sea, it is called a "typhoon".

A general name for both is "tropical storms".

What makes a Wind ?

Natasha asked - "What makes a wind, ma'am ?"

Ma'am replied - "A wind is simply the motion of air over the earth. What causes the air to move ? It's a change in the temperature, which causes all kinds of winds.

Whenever air is heated, it expands. This makes it lighter which then rises. As it rises, cooler air flows in to take its place. And this movement of air is called wind.

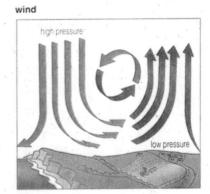

wind

There are two kinds of winds—those that are part of world-wide system of winds and local winds. Major wind systems of the world begin at the Equator, where the sun's heat is the maximum. Here, the heat rises to high altitudes and is pushed off towards the North and South poles. When it has journeyed about one-third of the distance to the poles, it has cooled and begins to fall back to earth. Some of this air returns to the Equator to be heated again and some continues on to the poles.

These global winds which are called "prevailing winds" are often broken up by local winds which blow from different directions. Local winds may be caused by the coming of cold air masses with high pressure or warmer air masses with low pressure. Local winds usually do not long last. After a few hours or at the most a few days, the prevailing wind pattern is present again. Other local winds are caused by the daily heating and cooling of the ground. Land and sea breezes are examples of this kind of wind."

What is a Monsoon ?

Dhritiman asked - "Ma'am, what is a monsoon ?"

Ma'am replied - "The word "monsoon" comes from an Arabic word meaning "season". It has to do with a type of climate in which wind blow from sea to land (onshore) during the warm season and from land to sea (offshore) during the cool season. The warm season of onshore winds is often very rainy while the cool season of offshore winds may be dry.

What causes this seasonal change in winds and rainfall? It is due to the fact that large continents or land masses heat and cool more rapidly than the surrounding oceans. Central and southern Asia grow warm rapidly in the spring and during the summer they are much warmer than the Indian ocean on the south or the Pacific Ocean on the east.

The warmer temperature inland create lower atmospheric pressures and therefore the wind blows inland from the surrounding seas. This is the onshore or summer monsoon.

In the autumn, interior Asia cools rapidly and during the winter it has much lower temperatures than the surrounding oceans. These lower temperatures create high atmospheric pressures, and therefore the winter monsoon winds blow outward from the dry interior regions toward the sea."

What causes Hail ?

Kihu asked - "Ma'am, what causes hail ?"

Ma'am replied - "Hail is formed when raindrops freeze while passing through a belt of cold air on their way to earth. Single raindrops form very small hailstones. But an interesting thing can happen to such a raindrop. As it falls as a hailstone, it may meet a strong rising current of air. So it is carried up again to the level where raindrops are falling. New drops begin to cling to the hailstone. And as it falls once more through the cold belt, these new drops spread into a layer around it and

freeze and now we have larger hailstones.

This rising and falling of the hailstone may be repeated time after time until it has added so many layers that its weight is heavy enough to overcome the force of the rising current of air. Now it falls to the ground.

This is the way, hailstones measuring 8 to 10 centimetres in diameter and weighing as much as 450 grams are sometimes built up. A hailstorm usually occurs during the warm weather and is accompanied in many cases by thunder, lightning and rain."

Why is it warmer in Summer ?

Sahara asked - "Ma'am, why is it warmer in summer ?

Ma'am replied - "You will be surprised to know that the earth is about 3,000,000 miles nearer to the sun in our northern winter than it is in summer. Yet it is much warmer in summer.

It is due to the slant of the earth's axis as it moves around the sun. The Equator of the earth is tilted 23½ degrees to the path of the earth around the sun.

The earth's axis always points towards the North Star as it moves around the sun. For this reason, during part of the year the North pole tilts towards the sun and part of the year away from it. When the North pole is inclined towards the sun, the Northern hemisphere has its summer. And when the North pole is inclined away from the sun, the Northern hemisphere has its winter. In the Southern hemisphere, these seasons are reversed.

In winter, the sun's rays are more slanting than in summer. Slanting rays produce

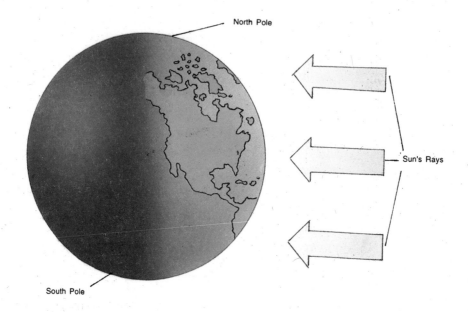

less heat because they scatter their heat over a larger area of the earth's surface. Moreover they lose more of their heat in passing through the atmosphere.

Due to the less slanting of sun rays in summer, its warmer in summer. There are other factors like water, land and altitude which help regulate the climate".

What makes the Weather ?

Rajiv asked - "Ma'am What makes the weather ?"

Ma'am replied - "Weather is just a condition of the air that surround us at any time. No matter what the air is — cold, cool, warm, hot, calm, breezy, windy, dry, moist or wet — that's weather.

Weather may be any combination of different amounts of heat, moisture and motion in the air. And it changes from hour to hour, day to day, season to season and even from year to year.

The daily changes are caused by storms and fair weather moving over the earth. The seasonal changes are due to the turning of the earth around the sun. The most important "cause" of weather is the heating and cooling of the air. Heat causes the winds as well as the different ways in which water vapour appears in the atmosphere.

Moreover, humidity combined with the temperature causes many weather conditions. Clouds and rains are all kinds of weather. Snow and hail are different phases of a weather."

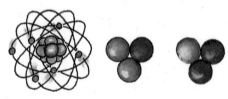

Who discovered the Atom?

Who invented the Typewriter?

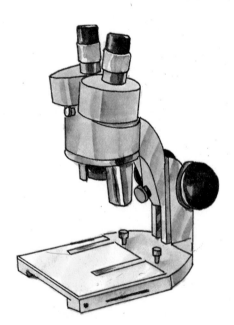

Who invented the Microscope?

Who made the first Photograph?

Who invented the Drum?

How Things Began ?

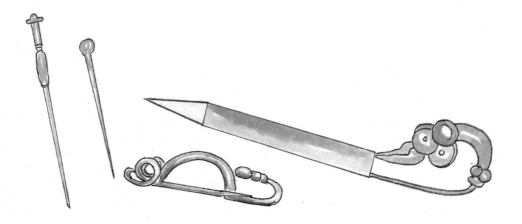

How did Pins originate?

What was the first Musical Instrument ?

Shubho asked - "Ma'am what was the first musical instrument ?"

Ma'am replied - "It's very difficult to say what the first musical instrument was. In fact we can never trace it because all over the world, all primitive people seemed to have made music of some sort. Music had a religious significance for them and they all danced, clapped hands and sang together.

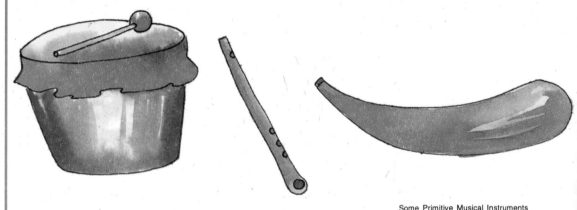

Some Primitive Musical Instruments

The first instrument might have been the ancestor of the present drum. Perhaps as they clapped hands to keep rhythm of song and dance, they began to drum on wood, or the earth. And gradually a drum kind of an instrument evolved. Later they made wind instruments, made from the horns of animals. Those instruments over the centuries developed into the modern brass instruments.

As the musical sense became sharper, reeds were used which

produced more natural tones. And then, the use of strings was discovered and as lyre and harp were invented, instruments were developed which were played with a bow.

In course of time, variety of instruments were invented by combining the old ones, by inventing further new ones."

When were Bells first made ?

Sanjeev asked - "When were bells first made, ma'am ?"

Ma'am replied - "It is rather impossible to trace the origin of bells.

For instance, more than 4,000 years ago, the Chinese had an instrument that consisted of 16 flat stones suspended in a frame and this gave forth a scale of exotic notes when struck by a wooden mallet. The Ancient Greeks and Romans had bells of all kinds, including hand bells. In Athens, they were used by priests and in Sparta, women walked in the streets striking small bells when a king died.

As the bell developed from its most primitive form, it went in two directions : one was the Eastern and the other was Western. In the Orient, the bell developed into forms that are "pot" and "bowl". The bowl became the gong, which is distinctively an oriental instrument. The pot developed into the Chinese and Japanese "barrel-formed" bells.

In western civilisation, the bell developed in a "cup" form and later it had a clapper so it could be struck from the inside. The large copper or bronze kettle mounted upside down atop a church was developed about the year 400."

Who invented the Piano ?

Rohan asked - "Ma'am, who invented the piano ?"

Ma'am replied - "Piano, one of the most complex musical instrument, began with a very simple instrument called "the monochord". It is not known who had invented the monochord. This was a box with a single string which had the intervals the scale marked on it. The player plucked the strings with a pick.

It was about the year 1,000 AD, Guido d' Arezzo invented a movable bridge for the monochord and added keys and more strings. This instrument was generally used until the 16th century.

From this instrument developed other stringed instruments like clavichord, spinet. In the middle of the 17th century, an instrument that became popular was the harpsichord. It is a larger instrument and had two keyboards. In shape, it is like a grand piano. Its strings are twanged by tiny quills.

Finally in 1709, Bartolommeo Christo Pori introduced the hammer action which sets the piano apart from earlier stringed instruments. This is the way piano was developed over the years. The proper name for the piano is "the pinoforte" which means "soft-strong" and which suggests the variety of tones the piano is capable of producing."

Who invented the Accordion ?

Megha asked - "Ma'am, who invented the accordion ?"

Ma'am replied - "The first instrument that was the ancestor of the modern accordion was produced and patented by an Austrian called Damian in 1829. It was called Piano accordion and was well known in European countries only until 1910. Gradually it spread to other countries. It has been developed in many ways since that time and in 1937 it was used for the first time in a Symphony Orchestra.

The accordion has 120 bass keys on one side and 41 treble keys on the piano type keyboard. It is an instrument made on the principle of the bellows. The sound is made by forcing air through metallic reeds.

The development of this instrument can be traced over a period of many years. The metal reeds, that are part of the instrument, were first used by the Ancient Chinese in a musical instrument known as a "Cheng". In the 16th century, the idea of putting wooden frame on bellows was originated. Keyboard are an invention that goes back to the 12th century."

Who invented the Drum ?

Disha asked - "Ma'am, who invented the drum ?"

Ma'am replied - "It is difficult to say who had invented the drum, since it is this instrument which had been in use since the earliest times. Many different kinds of drums have been used all over the world by the most primitive people. The drums were made of various materials like hollow tree trunks with animal skins stretched over them. Or bamboo drums made of long sections of the hollow reed, slit and beaten with sticks. Some people even used to beat their own bodies on the ground to produce a drum like sound !

American Indian Drum

The ancient Egyptians used drums and the typical Egyptian drum was small and was carried about in hand.

The American Red Indians not only used the drum to send messages and to mark time for their dances but they used drums to predict the weather ! When rainy weather approached, the skins that covered their drums would become taut."

How was the first Recording made ?

Debabrata asked - "Ma'am, how was the first recording made ? And who did it ?"

Ma'am replied - "The first recording was made by Thomas Edison in 1877. His first machine had a cylinder turned by a hand crank. There was also a horn and a blunted needle or "stylus". At the small end of the horn, there was a flexible cover. Sound waves that entered the large end of the horn moved this cover one way or another. To this the stylus was attached. It moved up and down with the sound waves.

A layer of tin foil covered the cylinder. The stylus pressed against this foil and gears moved the horn with its attached stylus slowly along the cylinder, as the crank was turned. In this way, as the stylus went around the cylinder many times, it made a crease in the tin foil.

The stylus moved up and down when someone sang or spoke into the horn. The stylus made a deeper groove in the tin foil when it was down, a lighter crease when it was in an upward position. The changing depth of the groove was the pattern of the sound waves made by a person singing or talking. It was the record of the sound.

To play the record, the stylus and horn were moved back to the begining of the groove. As the stylus followed the groove, it caused the flexible cover in the horn to vibrate in the same pattern. This made the air in the horn move to and fro and this made a sound like the original sound recorded !"

Who made the first Photograph ?

Ayesha asked - "Ma'am, who made the first photograph ?"

Ma'am replied - "Today when you snap a picture and have it developed so easily, it's hard to believe that hundreds of years of experimenting were needed before this became possible. It was not invented by any single person.

William Talbot

Between the 11th and 16th centuries, people had "the camera obscura" which enable them to show on paper an image which could be traced by hand to give accurate drawings of natural scenes. It didn't really "take" a picture. In 1568, Daniello Barbaro fitted the camera obscura with a lens and a changeable opening to sharpen the image. In 1802, Thomas Wedgewood and Sir Humphrey Davy recorded silhouettes and images of paintings on coated paper by contact printing, but they could not make the prints permanent.

In 1816, Joseph Niepce made a photographic camera with which he could get a negative image.

And in 1835, William Tolbot was able to obtain permanent images. Talbot was the first to make positives from negatives, the first to make enlargements by photography and the first to publish (in 1844) a book illustrated with photographs.

More and more developments were contributed by individuals all over the world as time went on. The popular Kodak box camera was placed in the market in 1888 and photography, as we know today, was on its way."

Who made the first Printing Press ?

Linda asked - "Ma'am, who made the first printing press ?"

Ma'am replied - "It was the Chinese and the Japanese who did the first kind of printing in the 15th century.

A method was needed to shorten the long labour of hand carving each page. It took many years while many people were at work on the problem.

Johann Gutenberg, a German printer living in Mainz, is generally believed to be the man who first solved the problem. He hit upon the idea of using movable metal type. He printed his first book, the famous Gutenberg Bible, by this method between 1453 and 1456.

Gutenberg's type was cast in a mould, each letter separately. When taken out of the mould, the type could be easily assembled or "set" in words, lines and pages. Once set and printed, the set were broken up and the letters reset and used again to print other pages.

This system is still in use today though later inventors have greatly speeded up the way in which the type is cast and set."

Who invented the Typewriter ?

Rishi asked - "Ma'am, who invented the typewriter ? It must be this century's invention, isn't it ?"

Ma'am replied -"You will be surprised that a patent for a typewriter was given to an Englishman called Henry Mill as long as 1714 ! Though this typewriter got never manufactured, we can get an idea how old the idea was. And the development of the typewriter was the work of many men, each contributing to the final one.

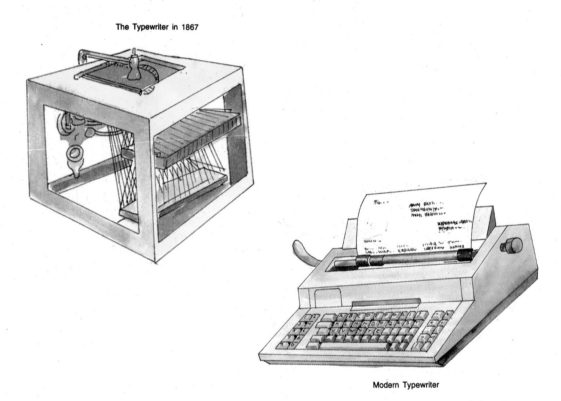

The Typewriter in 1867

Modern Typewriter

In the begining, the typewriters were patented as devices to aid the blind. In the USA, the first typewriter was patented by William Burt in 1829. In 1833, a French man, Xavier Progin invented a machine which used type bars with a key lever for each letter. In 1843, an American, Charles Thurber, patented a machine which made use of a set of type bars placed around a brass wheel. The wheel moved on a central pivot. It was brought around by hand to the letter desired, and the inked type struck directly upon the paper below. This was too slow a method.

The first practical type writer was the work of three US based inventors. They were

Christopher Sholes, Samuel Soule and Carlos Gliddon. It was in 1873.

And now we have portable typewriters, noiseless typewriters, electric typewriters and electronic typewriters with memories."

When were the first Coins made ?

Anupama asked - "Ma'am, when were the first coins made ?"

Ma'am replied - "The first coins were made in the 17th century B.C. by the Lydians who were a wealthy and powerful people living in Asia Minor. These coins were made of "electrum" which is a natural composition of 75% gold and 25% silver. They were about the size and shape of a bean and were known as "staters" or "standards"

Roman Coins

The Greeks started making coins when they saw the "staters". About 100 years later, many cities on the mainland of Greece and Asia Minor, on the island of the Aegean Sea and Sicily and in Southern Italy had coinages of their own. Gold coins were the most valuable. Next came silver and finally copper.

Greek coinage lasted for about 500 years. The Romans adopted the idea and carried it on for about another 500 years. Then the art of coinage declined and from the year 500 to about 1400, coins were thin and unattractive. But in the 15th century, it revived. Metal became plentiful. The first British coins were struck in the 18th century."

How did Pins originate ?

Rahul asked - "Ma'am, how did pins originate ?"

Ma'am replied - "The earliest form of a pin was perhaps a thorn. In fact the word "pin" resembles the Latin word for "thorn" which is "spina". Later on, people learned how to make pins out of the bones of fish or animals. In prehistoric times, Neolithic people were already making pins out of bronze.

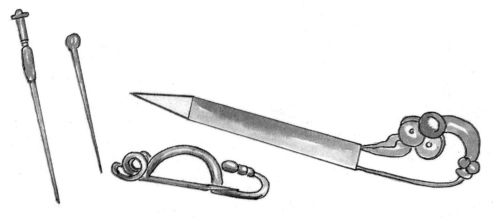

Early Bronze Pins

At the close of the Bronze age, a pin, very much like a safety pin, seems to have been in use in Europe. That was about 1000 B.C. It was made of bronze, very slender and bent in such a way that the point was caught against the head.

In Europe, pins were used in very early times, as a piece of decoration, rather than for fastening clothes. It was in the end of the 15th century that pins as we know them now began to be manufactured. They were considered so precious and so valuable that they made a new year's gift !

The first people to make modern type pins were the French who exported them to England. Gradually pins began to be produced almost all over the world."

When was Gas first used ?

Ruchira asked - "Ma'am, when was gas first used ?"

Ma'am - "Gas could be obtained from places where nature has stored away. Or it could be manufactured.

In 1792, a Scottish engineer called William Murdock was the first to use manufactured gas. He purified the gas that escaped from burning coal and piped it off to use for lighting his home. Later, he used it to light a factory in Birmingham.

In USA, manufactured gas was used for lighting before natural gas. In 1812, David Melville of Newport, Rhode Island, lit his home and the street in front with gas that he made from burning coal. In 1816, Baltimore, Mary Land lighted its streets with manufactured gas.

In 1821, natural gas was first used at Fredonia, New York.

Today it's the natural gas which is more in use than manufactured gas."

Who discovered the Atom ?

Priya asked - "Ma'am, who discovered the atom ?"

Ma'am replied - "It was an English chemist and mathematician called John Dalton who was the first man to have developed a scientific atomic theory in 1803. Till then, the idea of what matter or substance was, was something only philosophers thought about. As we know today, the atom is built on scientific

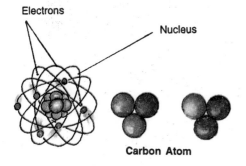

Carbon Atom

investigations of theories.

Dalton weighed samples of many gases, solids and liquids and found that they were all made up of unbelievably tiny particles which he too called atoms.

Almost a hundred years later, Ernest Rutherford, another Englishman, developed a theory about the atom which was like a description of a solar system : a heavy nucleus in the center with electrons, protons and neutrons.

Today, scientists have found more than 20 different particles in the core of the atom!"

Who invented the Thermometer ?

Aman asked - "Ma'am, who invented the thermometer ?"

Ma'am replied - "It was Galileo, the Italian scientist who made certain experiments around 1592. He made a kind of thermometer which is really called "an air thermoscope." It measured heat by measuring the expansion and contraction of air in a tube. So it was discovered that one of the problems with this thermometer was that it was affected by variations of atmospheric pressure and therefore wasn't complete accurate.

The type of thermometer we use today uses the expansion and contraction of a liquid to measure temperature. This kind of thermometer was first used about 1654 by the Grand Duke Ferdinand II of Tuscany.

The word "thermo" means heat and "meter" means measure. So a thermometer measures heat."

Who invented the Microscope ?

Sweta asked - "Ma'am, is magnifying glass a microscope ?"

Ma'am replied - "A magnifying glass is a simple microscope. By microscope, we generally mean "the compound microscope" in which magnification takes place in two stages. There is a lens called "the objective" which produces a primary magnified image.There is another lens called "the eyepiece" or "ocular", which magnifies that first image. There are actually several lenses used for both the objective and ocular but the principle is that of two stage magnification.

The word microscope is a combination of two Greek words, "mikros" or "small" and "skopos" or "watcher". So it is a "watcher of the small."

Who invented the microscope ? Galileo, the Italian scientist, invented it between 1590 and 1610. A Dutch scientist called Leeuwenhoek made many discoveries with the microscope. He showed that fleas and other minute creatures come from eggs. He was the first to see such microscopic forms of life as the bacteria and protozoa. And he was the first to see the whole circulation of the blood."

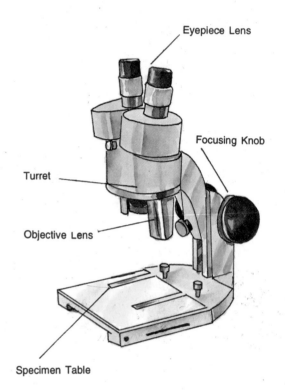

Eyepiece Lens

Focusing Knob

Turret

Objective Lens

Specimen Table

Who started Vaccination ?

Ma'am said - "I will tell you a very interesting story about vaccination.

It was in 1768 when small pox killed so many lives. There was a young medical student called Edward Jenner who overheard a remark made by a milkmaid. The milkmaid was telling somebody that she would not catch small pox as she already had cowpox. Cowpox was a disease with symptoms similar to those of small pox though in very much milder form.

Edward Jenner kept on thinking about the remark during his medical studies in London. In 1773, he qualified to be a doctor and came back to his native village in Gloucestershire to practice and to research. After 20 years of investigation and research, he found that the milkmaid had been right : those people who had cowpox, very rarely caught small pox.

In 1796, he gave people a light dose of cowpox to protect them from small pox. In 1798, he made his first really crucial test. Four children, who had been inoculated with cowpox were now inoculated with small pox. To his great joy, not one of them caught the dreaded disease. He had made the great discovery of vaccination, which has completely wiped out this dreaded disease."

Who was the first Astronaut ?

Tarini asked - "Who was the first astronaut ?

Ma'am replied - "Yuri Gargarin was the first man into space. In 1961, Russia took the world by surprise by launching the first man into space-Yuri Gargarin who completed a circuit of the earth in free fall.

As early as 1903, the Russian pioneer K.E.Tsiolkovsky suggested using rockets for space research, since rockets function by reaction motors and do not depend on a surrounding atmospheric medium. He also suggested liquid propellants because solid propellants were too weak and hard to control. In 1926, the first modern type liquid-propellant rocket was sent by R.H. Goddard in America. In Germany,

intensive research was undertaken, culminating in the liquid-propellant V_2 rocket, which bombarded England during the second world war.

After the war, serious work on the future development of rocket travel continued in the USSR and USA.

Before the Americans were ready to send up their first orbital satellite, Sputnik I was sent up from the Soviet Union."

Who first flew Kites ?

Jyotish asked - "Ma'am, who first flew kites ?"

Ma'am replied - "No one know who was the first to have flown kites. In the oriental countries, kites were probably flown first. In China, kites have always been an important part of many celebrations. On the ninth day of the ninth month, there is a big celebration called "The feast of high flight." The sky is dotted with kites of all shapes and sizes. Some are in the shape of fishes, frogs, birds. In India, we generally fly kites on the 14th of January. There are even "kite fights."

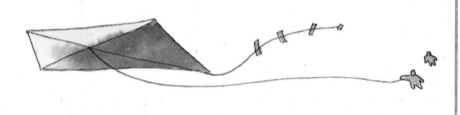

In western countries, kites have been used for different purposes. Thermometers have been attached to kites to learn the temperature of the clouds. Benjamin Franklin flew a silk kite in a thunderstorm and he used it to prove that lightning and electricity are the same thing. That was in 1752. By the end of 19th century, kites were being used by most weather bureaus. Some of these kites were sent up to heights of over four miles ! And for that, more then one kite was used, all attached together. The kite string was made of piano wire so light that a mile of it weighed only 7 kilograms and strong enough to lift 110 kilograms without breaking.

Before the airplane was invented, kites were also used for military purposes. For instance, one kite was 11 metres long and lifted a man 30 metres in the air !"

What is trial by Jury ?

Henry asked - "What is meant by trial by jury ?"

Ma'am replied - "When a crime is committed, the accused is produced before a jury. Twelve members of the trial jury listen to the evidence given by the witnesses, to the arguments of the lawyers, to the instructions of the judge. They then retire to a room to decide on their verdict. The 12 jurors are from all the walks of life. Henry II had decided the numbers of jurors in 1166 and ever since, it has been that way.

Before Jury trials, trials were conducted in different ways : in one method, an accused person brought into the court a number of neighbours who were willing to swear that he/she was innocent. The second method was "trial by ordeal" in which the accused was subjected to all kinds of ordeals like plunging his/her hands into burning oil or carrying a piece of hot iron ! If he survived the ordeal, he was declared innocent !

The third method was "trial by combat". Here a man had to do battle and defeat his enemy. If he won, he was innocent !

Trial by jury got rid of all these terrible methods."

Why do we have Gravestones ?

Linda asked - "Ma'am, why do we have gravestones ?"

Ma'am replied - "Thousands and thousands of years ago, people were more terrified of evil spirit. They thought that by using a stone to mark the grave of dead, they would keep the evil spirits, that were supposed to be in dead bodies, from rising up. The gravestones were also used to warn the people away from the spot. And then there were communities who put a gravestone on the spot so that nobody would dig the ground to plant trees or to irrigate the land.

The Egyptians built great tombs and pyramids to mark the places where their dead were burried. They kept all the favourite things of the dead inside the tomb and pyramid so that the dead could enjoy them even "after life". The Greeks ornamented their gravestones with sculpture. The Hebrews marked their graves with stone pillars. The Christians put a cross on the grave to keep the evil spirit away from the dead. To pay homage to the spirit of the dead, they have the practice of marking the graves."

What is Alcohol?

What is Ventriloquism?

What is Metal?

What is Ammonia?

What is Aluminium?

How Things Are Made?

What is Uranium?

Why is there lead in Petrol ?

Dheeraj asked - "Ma'am, why is there lead in petrol ?"

Ma'am replied - "To understand why there is lead in petrol, we have to first know what petrol is and how does it function.

Petrol is a mixture of hydrocarbons. These are substances composed of hydrogen and carbon atoms. The petrol, sold as motor fuel, is usually a blend of several different hydrocarbon liquids. Special substances, called additives, are mixed with the petrol to make it burn better.

Petrol turns into vapour from liquid at temperatures about 21 degrees centigrade. In an automobile engine, the gasoline is mixed with air and sprayed into the engine. The heat in the engine turns it into vapour. A spark plug then sets off a spark that burns the mixture.

Sometimes the petrol mixture may be ignited too soon. When this happens, the engine makes a sound, usually called a knock. There are two ways to reduce this engine knock. One is to use a slow burning petrol. The other is to put a chemical into the fuel to slow down the burning. The best known chemical used for this is called tetraethyl lead or simply ethyl. This is why there is "lead" in petrol."

How does heat Insulation work ?

Miku asked - "Ma'am, how does heat insulation work ?"

Ma'am replied - "Heat insulation slows down the flow of heat from one place to another. Different materials conduct heat differently. Some materials allow heat to flow through them easily while others prevent the movement of heat. For instance, silver is a good conductor of heat. It conducts heat about 19,300 times better than air does.

One of the best and most commonly used insulating materials is rock wool. It prevents the movement of heat (that is, it insulates) about 44 times better than glass, seven times better than wood and four times better than asbestos.

Heat insulation is very useful. It keeps a house comfortable in winter by keeping the heat in and in summer by keeping the heat out. It is also used on hot pipes and tanks to keep them from losing heat ; in refrigerators and cold-storage rooms to keep heat out."

What is Asbestos ?

Nishi asked - "Ma'am, what is asbestos ?"

Ma'am replied - "Asbestos" is a Greek word which means "inextinguishable". Today we apply the term to a group of fibrous minerals which have the property of resisting fire. The minerals that make up asbestos differ widely in composition and each has a different strength, flexibility and usefulness. From the chemical point of view, asbestos usually consists of silicates of lime and magnesia and sometimes contains iron.

Asbestos is found in certain types of rocks and sometimes it's necessary to mine and treat as much as 45 tonnes of rock to get one tonne of asbestos fiber !

Asbestos is similar to cotton and wool because it is made up of fibers. But asbestos has the added advantage of being heat and fire-resistant. This makes it very valuable for many uses in industry, and science has not yet been able to find a substitute for it.

No other mineral we know can be spun into yarn or thread, woven into cloth, or made into sheets. Workers in plants who are exposed to risks of fire sometimes wear complete outfits made of asbestos, including helmets, gloves, suits and boots.

Asbestos can withstand temperatures of

1,090 to 1,650 degrees centigrade, and there are some kinds of asbestos that can even resist temperatures as high as 2,760 degrees !"

What is Gypsum ?

Rahul asked - "Ma'am, what is gypsum ? I read that it is being used to make wall board and tiles because it resists fire and water so well."

Ma'am replied - "Yes, gypsum insulates a building against both heat and cold. It is a mineral of calcium sulphate in combination with water. There is a translucent kind of gypsum that is known as "selenite" and another that has a special lustre that is called "alabaster". Most gypsum is mined from thick beds. Some deposits of it are near the surface while others are far below.

Gypsum has been used as a plaster and a building material since the time of the ancient Egyptians. If gypsum is used alone or mixed with sand or lime, it can be moulded into casts, stucco, tiling, or finishing plasters.

Many stage and film-sets are made of gypsum wall boards and Plaster of Paris. Sculptors, surgeons and dentists also use it for making casts."

What is Metal ?

Ranvir asked - "Ma'am, what is metal ?"

Ma'am replied - "Physically, a metal is a substance that has a bright lustre and is a good conductor of heat and electricity. Metals have varying degrees of hardness, density, malleability and ductility. Malleability means it can be rolled out and hammered. Ductility has to do with being drawn out into wire.

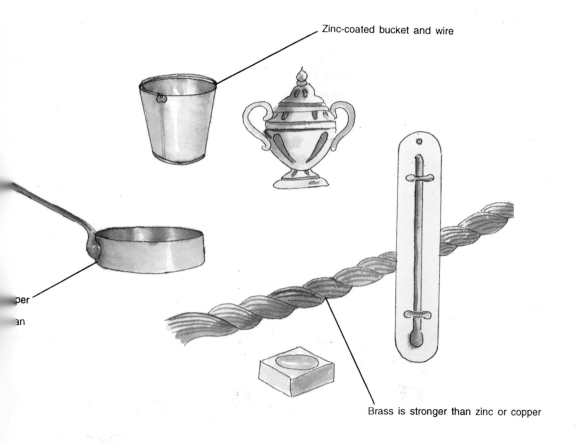

Zinc-coated bucket and wire

per
an

Brass is stronger than zinc or copper

Metal has a definite melting point and will fuse with other metals to form "alloys". With the exception of mercury, all metals are solids at ordinary temperature.

Some metals are found in the pure state but most of them are found in combination with other elements. These metals are in the form of sulphides, oxides, carbonates and silicates, usually mixed with rock and earthy materials, Some of the common metals found in combination in ores are lead, zinc, copper, iron, chromium, nickel and mercury. Some metals are so rare that tonnes of ore must be treated to get even a small amount of the pure metal. Radium is one of these. The science of recovering metals from their ores is called "metallurgy".

There are a few metals which, in small amounts, are necessary to animal life. Among these are iron, potassium, calcium, magnesium and sodium. A body even uses minute quantities of copper, aluminium and manganese !"

What is Aluminium ?

Gurjeet asked - "Ma'am, What is aluminium ?"
Ma'am replied - "Aluminium is a silvery-white metal that is only about one-third as heavy as iron. It can be drawn out in to wires that are finer than the finest hairs and hammered into sheets as thin as a sheet of newspaper. It may surprise you that it is the most abundant of all the metals in the world. Nearly 8% of the earth's crust is aluminium!

Aluminium is always found combined with various substances to form parts of many rocks and soils. The problem was how to separate aluminium from other substances. It was in 1886, on 23rd February, a twenty two year old chemist named Charles Martin Hall found a way to make this metal cheaply and in large quantities.

Aluminium is an almost perfect material for cooking utensils because it is a good conductor of heat and is easily kept clean and bright. It is also used in motor-car engines, aeroplanes and train engines.

Did you know that sapphires, rubies, garnets and other beautiful gems are compounds of aluminium ?"

What is Platinum?

Shella asked - "What is platinum ?"
Ma'am replied - "Platinum is a metal. It is greyish white in colour and its name comes

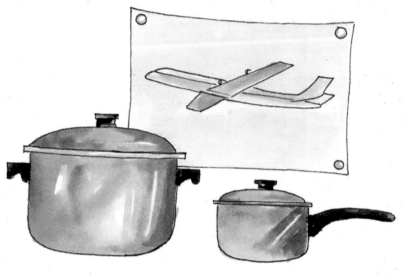

from the spanish "Plata" and means "little silver". Platinum is harder than copper and almost as pliable as gold.

While the chief use of platinum is for jewellery, it is also used for contact points where electrical circuits are opened or closed, in laboratory weights, in instruments for exact measurement of temperatures and for fuses in delicate electrical instruments.

What makes platinum especially useful is that it resists oxidation, acids and heat. The melting point of platinum is about 1,843 degrees centigrade. For most purposes, it is mixed (alloyed) with one of the other "platinum metals" or with silver, gold, copper, nickel or tin. Platinum is almost twice as heavy as lead.

Platinum is usually found in ores often mixed with the rare metals palladium, rhodium, iridium, osmium which are called "platinum metals". Occasionally it is found with metals such as gold, copper, silver, iron, chromium and nickel. It is found in the form of small grains, scales or nuggets."

What is Uranium ?

Dorothy asked - "Ma'am, What is uranium ?"

Ma'am replied - "Uranium is a metal, an ore and one of the heaviest elements. When you look at clean pure uranium metal, it is as shiny as silver. But after a few minutes of exposure to air, the uranium surface becomes dull and turns brown. The film that forms is uranium and oxygen. And it serves to protect the metal underneath.

Uranium has natural radioactivity and this is the biggest difference between uranium and other metals. Radioactivity means the metal slowly changes by giving off certain rays that come out of the atom of the uranium. They are called alpha, beta and gamma rays.

By giving off radiation, the uranium atom changes and becomes another radioactive element. This element in turn changes by giving off more radiation. And this process goes on as long as a radioactive element is left.

There are 14 steps in this series. One of the steps produces radium and the last one produces lead. After that the series is ended because lead is not radioactive. To change from uranium to lead in nature takes billions of years ."

What is Fallout ?

Ravinder asked - "What is fallout ?"

Ma'am replied - "The dust and other materials that are in the air as the result of a nuclear explosion that is from atom bombs - is fallout. It poisons the air, soil and water. It poisons because it is radioactive. This means that it contains certain kinds of atoms that are breaking down. As they break down, they give off tiny amounts of energy and matter which are called "radiations".

A nuclear explosion produces a huge blast, a lot of heat and many radioactive atoms. These radioactive atoms become mixed with particles of soil and dust from the earth. Tonnes of radioactive dust are blown or sucked into the atmosphere by a nuclear explosion. This returns to the earth as radioactive fallout.

The heaviest particles of this debris drop to earth within minutes or a few hours of a nuclear explosion. The lighter particles are carried up and they come down more slowly. They may circle the earth for months or even years. And then they fall on the earth, mostly in snow, rain and mist.

Sometimes fallout enters the body with the air, water and food. Inside the body, radioactive atoms from the fallout send off radiations. When too much radiation passes through living cells,it may damage the cells or weaken the body's defences against disease."

What is Slate ?

Shabnam asked - "Ma'am, what is slate ?"

Ma'am replied - "Millions of years ago, fine - grained clay particles settled on the bottoms of lakes and inland seas and formed a soft mud. This later hardened into the mud -rock that is called "shale". During this period, the earth's crust moved and shifted. The layers of shale, covered by beds of other rocks, were folded up into wrinkles. These were flattened and squeezed so hard that the shale became slate.

The clay particles making up the slate were deposited by the lakes and seas in layers. Even after the pressure changed the shale to slate, the many separate layers of the deposits remained. And today we can split slate into wide, thin plates because it did stay in layers.

The most common colours of slate are dark grey and black, though it may also be red, green or various shades of grey. The reason it is chiefly black is that the living matter in the original muds left carbon material.

Slates occur only where mountain-making pressure and earth changes have been active upon the layers of old shale.

Slate is used for many purposes. One of its chief uses is as a roofing material for homes and buildings of all kinds. Among, other things made from slate are blackboards, table tops and draining boards."

What is Ammonia ?

Sudha asked - "Ma'am, What is ammonia ?"

Ma'am replied - "Ammonia is a colourless gas with a very strong odour. In fact, breathing in too much ammonia may cause death.

Traces of ammonia are found in the air, having come from the decay of animal and vegetable matter. Sometimes, it is found in minute quantities in rain water. But most of the ammonia used in commerce is artificially made.

Ammonia is composed of the elements nitrogen and hydrogen. If we combine these two gases, we can get ammonia. The nitrogen is obtained from the air and the hydrogen from the water. The two gases are dried, compressed, heated to a temperature of about 530 degrees centigrade and passed over a mixture of various salts, whereupon they combine to form ammonia.

When ammonia comes in contact with acids, it forms ammonium salts. Ammonium salts are very useful. Ammonium chloride is used in soldering, in dry cells and in medicine. Ammonium sulphate is a valuable fertilizer. Ammoniuim nitrate is used in fertilizers as well as in explosives. Smelling salts contain ammonium carbonate. Ammonia is about 3/5 as heavy as air."

What is an Acid ?

Mayankh asked - "Ma'am, acid is very harmful, isn't it ?"

Ma'am replied - "A very small number of acids are very harmful. There are many acids in foods and they are necessary for good health. Other acids are used to make drugs, paints, cosmetics and industrial products.

There are many kinds of acids but they all may be divided into two classes : inorganic acids and organic acids.

Organic acids are not as strong as the inorganic ones. Acetic acid is found in vinegar and can be made by fermenting apple cider. When sugar ferments in milk, lactic acid is formed. It turns the milk sour but it is used in making cheese. Amino acids are needed to keep the body in good health and they come from protein foods. Oranges, lemons, grapefruit contain ascorbic acid, which is the chemical name for vitamin C. Liver, poultry and beef contain nicotinic acid, which prevent skin diseases. The human body makes a small amount of weak hydrochloric acid, which helps in digestion.

Sulphuric acid, an inorganic acid, is an important industrial acid. It can cause severe damage to the eyes and serious burns on the skin. Nitric acid is another powerful acid which can harm the skin and eyes.

But all kind of acids are not harmful."

What is Chlorine ?

Juhi asked - "Ma'am, what is chlorine ?"

Ma'am replied - "Pure chlorine is a gas. It is one of the most deadly poisonous gases and also one of the most useful. In nature, chlorine is a part of compounds such as common salt (Sodium chloride).

A Swedish chemist called Karl Scheele prepared pure chlorine for the first time in 1774. It is now made cheaply by passing a current of electricity through a solution of common salt.

The first poison gas used during world war I was almost pure chlorine.

But chlorine is also one of our most useful weapons for health. It destroys germs as part of many germicides and disinfectants. Most city water-purification systems use chlorine to kill any bacteria that live through the treatment process. Only about four or five parts of the liquid chlorine per 1,000,000 parts of water are used. This amount is not harmful to us. "

What is Alcohol ?

Radhika asked - "Ma'am, what is alcohol ?

Ma'am replied - "There are actually many different alcohols. One of the most common type is the kind found in alcoholic drinks. This is "ethyl alcohol" and is usually known as "grain alcohol".

Grain alcohol is made from starches and

sugars and can be made from most vegetables, grains and fruits. It is generally made from corn, rye, barley. In Ireland, there is a famous alcoholic drink called "poteen" which is made from potatoes. When made from starch, the starch is first changed to sugar and the sugar is then fermented to give alcohol.

As a fuel, alcohol is very valuable. During World War II, various countries that lacked oil used alcoholic mixtures in place of petrol in cars.

Alcohol is often used as a solvent as in making varnishes for wood and lacquers for metals. It is also used in preparation of anaesthetics such as chloroform and ether and in the manufacture of many substances such as dyes, medicines, liniments and vinegar. When alcohol is taken into the body in small amounts, it unites with oxygen to give heat.

Did you know alcohol is an antiseptic, and that it is used in museums and hospitals to preserve specimens ?"

What is Ventriloquism ?

Amritya asked - "In ancient Greece, in Athens, there was a very famous ventri loquist called Eurycles. In Egypt, people thought that the statues spoke while actually it was done by ventriloquism. Ma'am, how is it done?"

Ma'am replied - "The word ventriloquism comes from the Latin "VENTER" meaning "belly" and "loqui" meaning "to speak" . A ventriloquist was

thought to be a belly-speaker. That is they thought a ventriloquist spoke using the stomach. But it is not true.

How does then a ventriloquist make the dolls speak ? A ventriloquist forms the words in a normal manner. But what he/she does is allow the breath to escape slowly, the tones are muffled and the mouth is opened as little as possible. The tongue is pulled back and

only the tip is moved. The pressure on the vocal cords to muffle the tones spreads the sound and the greater the pressure the greater is the illusion that the sound is coming from a distance.

The ventriloquist uses a dummy to turn our attention away from his/her own mouth. The mouth of the dummy moves while the ventriloquist's lips is kept still. That creates the impression that it is the dummy which is talking."

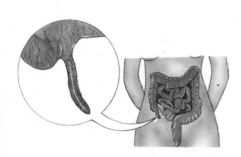

What is an Appendix?

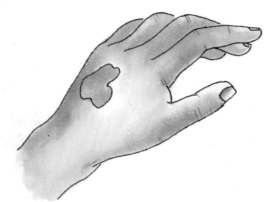

What are Birthmarks?

Human Body

What is Blood Transfusion?

What happens when we get Dizzy ?

Ruchira said excitedly - "Maa'm, we were going round and round in the corridor. And all of us couldn't continue it for long because we felt so dizzy. Why do we go dizzy ?"

Ma'am replied - "To understand why we go dizzy, we have to first understand what gives us a sense of balance. We have a sense of balance because we have three elongated tubes in the form of three semi-circular arcs, which are located behind our ears. These are called "semi-circular canals". These three canals are placed almost at right angles to each other in the three dimensions of space : length (backwards and forwards), breadth (right and left) and height (up and down).

In these canals, there is a fluid (lymph) and at one end of the tubes, they are enlarged into a bulb-shape called the "ampulla". In these ampullae, there are sensitive cells out of which grow stiff hairs. The hairs stick up into the space of the ampulla and are connected to nerve fibres.

Whenever the fluid in the canal moves, it makes the hairs move or bend and this sends a message to the brain and to the muscles. When we move forward, the canal which responds to motion in a forward or backward direction will cause the hairs in it to bend backward. The lymph in the canal causes this.

When you revolve rapidly in a circle, the lymph in the horizontal semi-circular canal bends the sensory hairs backward. When you stop, the lymph keeps going around because of inertia. This causes the hairs to bend in the opposite direction. And this makes you feel you are revolving in the opposite direction even though you are not. And this is what happens when you are dizzy."

How can we Balance ourselves on two legs ?

Satyajit asked - "How can we balance ourselves on two legs ?"

Ma'am replied - "You will be astonished to know that just to keep our balance as we stand still takes the work of about 300 muscles in our body ! Why do we feel tired when we stand for a long time ? It's because our muscles are constantly at work even when we stand still. When we stand still, we are performing a constant act of balancing. We change from one leg to the other, we use pressure on our joints.

When we walk, we not only use our balancing trick, but we also make use of two natural forces to help us. The first is air pressure. Our thigh bone fits into the socket of the hip joint so snugly that it forms a kind of vacuum. The air pressure on our legs helps keep it there securely. This air pressure also makes the leg hang from the body as if it had very little weight.

The second natural force we use in walking is the pull of the earth's gravity. After our muscles have raised our leg, the earth pulls it downward again and keeps it swinging."

Why does Alcohol make one drunk ?

Nishi asked - "Yesterday I saw two drunkards by the road side. They were shouting and laughing and their speech was slurred. They could not walk straight. Why does alcohol make one drunk ?"

Ma'am replied - "Alcohol is a narcotic. A narcotic is a substance which enters the nerve cells quickly and tends to paralyze them. But before it paralyzes, it stimulates nerve cells, putting them in a state of excitement. What happens is that action and speech seem to be speeded up. The skin gets redder, blood pressure rises, the heart beats faster and breathing is quickened. But alcohol soon has a depressing effect on the brain. The ability to observe, think and pay attention is affected. And as the higher functions of the brain are paralyzed, the power to control moods is lost.

Moreover, inhibitions are relaxed. In our body, nerve fibres called inhibitory fibres act as brakes in the nervous system. They are developed as a result of education and discipline. These inhibitory fibres get paralyzed by alcohol. And then people say and do things which they would never in a state of alcohol free mind. This is the reason why alcohol makes one drunk.

You must have noticed in many medicines, alcohol is being used. This is because alcohol acts as a stimulant first. If it is taken into the body in weak solutions, it will act as a stimulant and not as a narcotic."

What is Amnesia ?

Natasha asked - "One of my uncles could not remember his own name. And he didn't remember anything about his past either.But later, he recovered. They said he was suffering from amnesia. What is it, Ma'am ?"

Ma'am replied - "Amnesia is a state of loss of memory. It may be permanent or temporary. Your uncle suffered from a temporary attack of amnesia.

One type of amnesia may result from an injury to the head. The person remembers nothing about the accident. And if there has not been serious damage to the brain, memory usually returns within a few days.

Another kind of amnesia is called hysterical amnesia. It may happen when a person tries to remove himself/herself from a situation which is unbearable. The anxiety becomes so much that the person is forced to forget it. When anxiety is forgotten, the person may forget many other things including his/her own identity. This generally lasts a short time period. And later, one gets back one's memory."

How does the Brain help us to see ?

Peter asked - "Ma'am, it is not only our eyes but brain too which help us to see. isn't it ?" How does it happen ?"

Ma'am replied - "Seeing is done by the eye but our brain plays a very important part in this process.

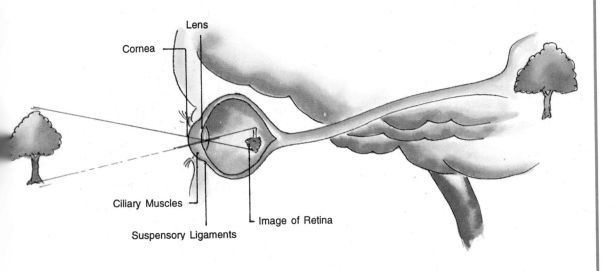

Lens
Cornea
Ciliary Muscles
Suspensory Ligaments
Image of Retina

When we look at an object, light waves pass through the lens of the eye and form an inverted image on the retina. The retina is a carpet-like screen of cells at the back of the eyeball. Each of the retina's 130,000,000 cells is sensitive to light. When light strikes a cell, a chemical change takes place. This starts an impulse in a nerve fibre which travels through the optic nerve to the seeing portion of the brain.

Now when we look at things, our eyes stop for only a second at the grass, bird, dog, car, squirrel, child. But the brain doesn't see a series of quick snap shots. It is the seeing part of the brain which records each picture and remembers it. It adds them together and gives them meaning so that the whole picture is seen, not the parts. In less than a second, it draws up on the store of memories in the brain.

We can say that seeing includes the use of many parts of the eye, the optic nerve and the parts of the brain that see and interpret the eye's messages."

What causes Deafness ?

Madhu asked - "Ma'am, what causes deafness ?"

Ma'am replied - "Deafness is caused by several factors. One may be born deaf due to some defect in the auditory nerve. One may become deaf due to an accident or illness. It is difficult to prevent deafness when one has some inborn defect. But when one has become deaf after an illness, one may recover in future.

Deafness means nearly complete or total loss of hearing. There are people who are hard of hearing. It means when some of the ability to hear is lost. It may be caused by an infection. Moreover head colds, tonsilitis, measles, scarlet fever, mumps and meningitis may cause poor hearing. There are cases when it is due to a bony growth in the ear, which makes it difficult for the sound wave to be conducted into the ear.

Now a days, it is caused by sound itself. If a person is exposed continuously to the sound of explosions, violent vibrations, the noises of heavy industrial machines, a slow and gradual loss of hearing may take place. This kind of deafness ranks third among all the causes of poor hearing. The violent sound waves affect part of the hearing mechanism and high tones can no longer be heard.

Moreover, changes may take place in the auditory nerve and lead to a partial loss of hearing after the age of 50."

Why does the nose have Mucus ?

Mayank asked - "Ma'am, why does the nose have mucus ?"

Ma'am replied - "The mucus in our nose guards our health ! We generally inhale millions of dust granules every minute of the day and night. This is true no matter where you live ! The only air that is dust-free is the air over the ocean once we get at least 600 miles from shore! Even a breath of pure country air contains about half a million dust particles. Along with dust, all types of bacteria enter our nose when we breathe. These bacteria stick to the mucus layer in our nose. And the mucus is antiseptic, it kills many of the bacteria.

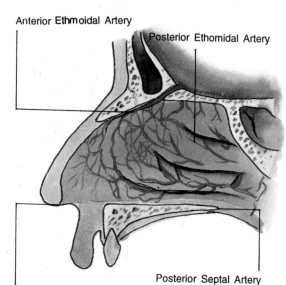

Anterior Ethmoidal Artery
Posterior Ethomidal Artery
Posterior Septal Artery
Mucous Membrane

The first cleaning of the air is carried by the bristle hairs which are at the entrance to the nose. The coarse dust particles are removed here. Starting with the nose and extending to the air chambers of the lungs, the passage way is lined with cells which have delicate little hairs growing out of them. These hairs are called "cilia".

The cilia brings dust granules from the windpipe and carry them into the nose where they become mixed with the mucus which kills the bacteria. The mucus which is as clear as glass becomes greyish green in colour. The mucus in our nose helps us a lot in keeping good health."

What are Fingernails made of ?

Archana asked - "Ma'am, why doesn't it pain when we cut our nails ?"

Ma'am replied - "This is because the nails are made up of dead cells. The nails are special structures that grow from the skin. Most of the nail is made up of a substance called "keratin". Keratin is a tough dead form of protein and a horn-like

material.

At the base of the nail, and part of the way along its sides, the nail is embedded in the skin. The skin beneath the nail is just like any other skin except that it contains elastic fibers. These are connected to the nails to hold it firmly.

Most of the nail is quite thick but at the point near the roots beneath the skin, it is very thin. This part is white in appearance and has the shape of a semicircle or half-moon. It is called the "lunule". The fingernails grow about 50 millimetres a years.

Some of us have brittle nails. This may be due to infections, a disturbance of the nutritional system, poor circulation of the blood or even glandular disturbances."

What causes Dandruff ?

Uma asked - "Ma'am, what causes dandruff ?"

Ma'am replied - "You will be surprised when I tell you even medical science does

not really know what causes dandruff !

It might be considered a disease of the scalp which produces small flakes on the scalp and in the hair. The scientific name for this condition is Seborrheic dermatitis.

Medical science believes that it may be caused by infection of some sort but the agent that might be causing such an infection has not yet been found.

When dandruff appears, certain glands which are connected to the roots of the hair, become overactive. These glands are called "sebaceous glands" and they produce an oily material called "sebum". This oily substance makes the scales or flakes greasy. And this can make scalp itchy.

There are times when in the dandruff full of area, there are more bacteria and fungi. If the dandruff produces an itching, through the scratches, germs may enter and cause infection.

Washing the hair at least once or twice a week and thorough massage do help remove the excess of oil and flakes."

Why do we get Pimples ?

Sahana asked - "Ma'am, I am fed up of pimples. Why do we get pimples ?"

Ma'am replied - "Do you know where does pimple start most often ? Pimples start most often in the follicles of the hair. Blackheads too start in there. There are certain glands called "sebaceous glands" which deposit an oily material there. When the hair follicle becomes plugged up and this deposit collects, it forms a blemish we call a blackhead. Pimples are small raised areas of the skin which often have pus in them.

Pimples may be caused by many conditions. An improper diet, a glandular imbalance or tiny infections in the skin may cause pimples.

There are times when pimples give us a sign that a more serious skin disorder is developing. It may be a sign of some diseased condition in the body also. A person should consult a doctor when he/she has many pimples on the body. One more important thing to remember is that pimples should never be squeezed. This makes it possible for bacteria to get into the area."

What are Birthmarks ?

Anup asked - "Ma'am, my mother tells me that I had a reddish stain on my skin when I was born. But now, I don't have that mark. Why did I have birthmarks ?"

Ma'am replied - "The reddish or purple stain that appear on the skin at birth are actually an unusual formation of blood vessels. These birthmarks disapppear without treatment.

The scientific name for a birthmarks is "NAEVUS" and it generally refers to a mole which is present at birth or develops shortly after birth. Medical science still does not know what causes them and neither does it know how to prevent their appearance.

We all have at least one mole somewhere on the body, including the scalp. They may vary greatly in appearance since this depends on the layer of skin in which they spring up. Most moles develop before or right after birth but in some cases they do not show up until one is about fourteen or fifteen.

Birthmarks do not generally cause serious physical problems, but they may be transformed into a cancerous growth. But that is very rare."

What is Ringworm ?

Samit asked - "What is Ringworm, ma'am ?"

Ma'am replied - "The medical name for ringworm is "TINEA". Ringworm or tinea is a very common disease of the skin. It is caused by a fungus infection.

Ringworm is usually seen on the arms and legs. The most common form of it is one or several raised round sores on the skin. They seem to heal in the centre while the edges continue to grow outward. Sometimes the healed centre part becomes reinfected.

A ringworm sore starts as a small slightly raised area with a reddish colour. Then it gets redder and there may be some blisters and a slight itching or burning sensation. It sometimes appear on scalp.

It is a very contagious disease and it is very difficult to destroy the fungi that causes ringworm. So treatment of the patient usually consists of trying to prevent the infection from spreading until it eventually ends."

Where do Warts come from ?

Manju asked - "Ma'am, where do warts come from ? Do they appear when we touch toads ?"

Ma'am replied -"We don't get warts by handling toads. Even dogs and cats have warts but no animal can pass warts on to human beings.

Warts are caused by a virus which is a very small germ. A wart is usually a small raised area of the skin which is quite rough or pitted on the surface. It is flesh-coloured or slightly darker than the normal skin. Since the wart is caused by a virus, it can be spread by scratching it and spreading the virus on the skin. That's why there are many warts on the skin.

We find that the most of the warts disappear after a year or two. But there is really no guarantee that they won't spread or continue on and on. The doctor usually uses some form of local medication. The doctor may inject special preparations into each wart. When there is constant pressure on a wart, such as those on the palms or soles, the problem becomes a bit more serious. It may become hardened and it may have to be removed."

What is Measles ?

Amrita asked - "What is measles ? Does it occur in childhood ?"

Ma'am replied - "Measles is generally a childhood disease but grown-ups who never had it may get it too. Measles is caused by a virus, a living germ, too small to see even in ordinary microscope.

It spreads very easily. The infection is spread by droplets in the air when a sick person coughs. About 10 to 12 days after contact with the virus, red spots appear in the throat and mouth. The temperature rises, the nose begins to run and a cough develops. One or two days later, a red rash breaks out all over the body. And the child has high fever. The whites of the eyes become inflamed and the eyes are sensitive to light.

When the rash has covered the entire body, the temperature drops suddenly and the child feels better. There is no special treatment for this disease. A serum can be used to weaken the force of the infection. The child needs a lot of rest and should be kept in a dark room.

Babies up to the age of about five months don't get measles if the mother has had the disease."

Why do children get Chicken Pox ?

Amrit asked - "Ma'am, why don't grown ups get chicken pox ?"

Ma'am replied - "The reason is that once a person has had an attack of chicken pox, it makes the person immuned to the disease. And so if one has got it in childhood, one is through with it.

Chicken pox is caused by a virus. It is very contagious. It is usually transmitted directly from person to person and not by contact with clothing or other articles soiled by an infected person. A child who has chicken pox can be considered infectious for about 14 days.

Some of the symptoms are a slight rise in temperature, loss of appetite, headache and backache. But sometimes the first sign of chicken pox is a rash or eruption of the skin. Since a person with chicken pox can infect another person about two days before the rash appears, you can see how a whole group of children could become infected before anything was done to prevent it.

Chicken pox is usually a mild disease but a doctor must observe the patient to see if there are any complications."

What causes Gout ?

Joyti asked - "Why was Gout thought of as a "rich man's disease ? What causes it ?"

Ma'am replied - "At one time it was believed that gout was caused by eating too much and drinking too much wine. And so, it was known as a rich man's disease.

Gout is a very painful disease. In 70% of the cases, the first attack is in the large toe and in 90% of the cases, the large toe is involved later on. The pain seems to come very suddenly. Within hours, the joint swells, becomes hot red and tender. It hurts so much that a person with gout is very much afraid of being touched on the painful part.

The painful condition lasts a few days or weeks and then disappears completely until the next attack. Physical strain, emotional strain, allergy also cause gout.

Gout is a condition of having too much uric acid in the blood. A person who has gout, is unable to break down certain proteins taken into the body. These proteins are called "purins" and are obtained from the diet of the person. Among the foods with a high purine content are : sweet bread, liver, kidney, sardines, turkey, pork, beef. A person with gout should avoid such food."

What is an Appendix ?

Vikram asked - "Ma'am, what is an appendix ? Why does it have to be removed when one gets appendicitis ?"

Ma'am replied - "The appendix is a hollow tube, about 8 to 15 centimetres long, closed at the end. It is a kind of off-shoot of the large intestine. The wall of the appendix has the same layers as the

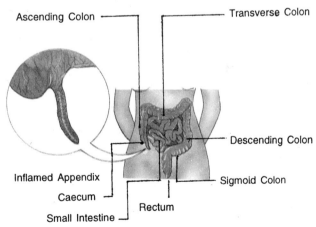

wall of the intestine. The inner layer gives off a sticky mucus. Beneath it is a layer of

69

lymphoid tissue. It is in this tissue that trouble may occur.

This tissue may become swollen when there is infection in the body. The contents of the intestine enter the appendix but are not easily forced out. If the tissue is swollen, the contents of the tube may remain inside and become hard. The veins of the appendix may be easily squeezed by the hardened material and swollen tissue. This cuts off the blood flow and may cause infection.

Appendicitis or inflammation of the appendix is very common. The symptoms are pain, tenderness and spasm in the right side of the abdomen. Sometimes the pain is first felt in the pit of the stomach and then is concentrated on the right side. Immediate operation has to be done which is very safe. The appendix is a part of the body that we can manage without."

What is the Spleen ?

Radhika asked - "Ma'am, what is the spleen ? If it is removed, can the body function properly ?"

Ma'am replied - "The spleen plays a part in making blood during childhood. It fights diseases of the blood and the bone marrow such as malaria and anaemia. If the spleen is removed from the body, these vital processes will go on being performed ! The other parts of the body take over the work of the spleen.

The spleen is a large organ in the abdomen and lies next to the stomach but it is not part of the digestive system. It is really attached to the bloodstream.

About ten million red blood cells are destroyed every second in a healthy human being. They are being replaced by the bone marrow, the liver and the spleen. Surplus red cells are stored in the spleen and old and worn-out red cells are broken down in the spleen.

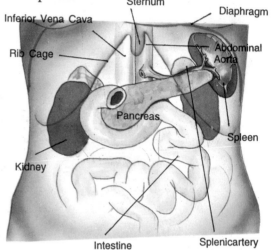

Moreover certain white cells called lymphocytes are manufactured in the spleen and in the marrow. When there is a sudden loss of much blood, the spleen releases large numbers of red cells to make up for the loss."

Is all Human Blood the same ?

Sarabjit asked - "Ma'am, is all human blood the same ?"

Ma'am replied - "Though all human blood is made up of basically the same plasma, cells and other chemical materials, everyone's blood isn't exactly the same. This is because our blood differs in some of the arrangements and proportions of the chemicals in their cells and plasma.

If a drop of one blood type is added

to the blood or serum of another type, the blood cells become clumped together. This is known as "agglutination" and this is followed by the destruction of blood cells. By means of agglutination tests, it has been found out that the blood of human beings can be divided into four groups : O, A, B and AB. This classification is based on the presence or absence of certain protein molecules in the blood.

The cells of group O are not agglutinated by the serum of any other group. So type O blood can be given to any person in a transfusion. This is the reason why people with type O blood are known as "universal donors". In group AB, the serum does not agglutinate any cells so that people with this blood type can recieve any other type of blood.

As we move from west to east, the percentage of people with blood type A decreases while B group grows larger. In England 43% belong to group A, in Russia, 30% and in India only 15%. When it comes to group B, the opposite is true."

Ma'am replied - "When a person looses a great deal of blood for some reason his/her life can often be saved by a blood transfusion. The blood of another person is put into the circulatory system which replaces the lost blood. One or two litres of new blood transfusion into the veins means new life to the patient.

Blood of the donors is typed in advance and in the blood banks of the hospitals, the blood is kept at low temperatures which is available instantly. Blood banks not only store blood, they also store "plasma". When the cells are removed from blood, the remaining "plasma" can be given to anyone no matter what one's blood group is. The liquid or plasma portion of the blood is separated from the blood cells and frozen. Then a drying process reduces the plasma to powder. This is packed in a sealed package accompanied by another container which has sterilized water. When blood is needed, the water restores the plasma to its original fluid state, ready for injection."

What is Blood Transfusion ?

Gurpreet asked - "Ma'am, what is blood transfusion ?"

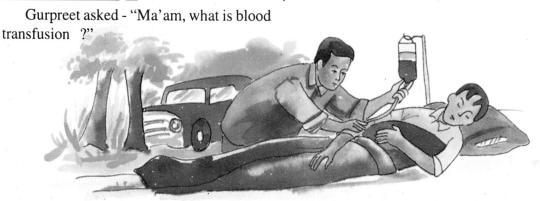

What is the Rh factor ?

Robert asked - "What is the Rh factor, ma'am?"

Ma'am explained - "In 1940, it was found that there was still another way of dividing blood into groups and this was according to the Rh factor. This discovery was made in the course of experiments on rhesus monkey and that's why it came to have the name "Rh".

It was found out that when certain combinations of blood were made, the red blood cells broke apart. The cause was traced to certain differences in the Rh factor.

The blood of human beings in this case is divided into Rh positive and Rh negative. When blood from an Rh positive person is transfused to a person who is Rh negative, the latter will develop a blood disease when he receives Rh positive blood again.

In rare cases (one in forty or fifty), an Rh positive father and Rh negative mother will produce an infant with a blood disease if certain other conditions exist."

How fast does our Blood flow ?

Piya asked - "Ma'am, how fast does our blood flow ?"

Ma'am replied - "The time needed for the blood to circulate through the entire body-that is from the heart to the lung to the heart to the body to the heart is about 23 seconds. A single blood cell makes about three thousand round trips through the body's circulation in one day.

Blood doesn't flow through the human body the way water flows through a regular series of pipes. The vessels through which blood is pumped out of the heart to all parts of the body are the arteries. But the arteries that are some distance from the heart keep on dividing and dividing until they become tiny vessels called capillaries. The blood flows much more slowly through these vessels than it does through arteries.

Capillaries are fifty times thinner than a human hair. The blood corpuscles pass through them in single file. A quantity of blood takes about one second to flow through a capillary.

Blood is constantly flowing through the heart and it takes about 1.5 seconds for a given quantity of blood to pass through the heart. Blood flows from the heart to the lung and back to the heart which takes about 5 to 7 seconds.

Blood flows from the heart to the brain and back to the heart. This takes about eight seconds. The longest trip the blood has to make is from the heart through the trunk and the legs to the toes and then back to the heart. This takes about 18 seconds.

The condition of the body has an effect on how fast the blood flows. For example fever or work can increase the number of heartbeats and make the blood flow twice as fast."

What makes the rate of Heartbeat change ?

Akilesh asked - "Ma'am, what makes the rate of our heartbeat change ?"

Ma'am replied - "You all know that each beat of the human heart lasts about 0.8 seconds. The heart beats about 100,000 times a day. It also rests an equal number of times between beats. In one year, the heart beats about 40,000,000 times.

What is exactly the beating of the heart ? It is really a wave of contraction that takes place in the heart to send blood circulating through the body. So the rate of the heartbeat (or pulse rate) depends on the body's need of blood.

Change in the heartbeat is most often caused by work. When a muscle begins to function somewhere in the body, it produces carbonic acid. The molecules of carbonic acid are carried by the blood to a certain part of the heart, the right atrium, within ten seconds.

There are cells there that react to the presence of the carbonic acid molecules. And the reaction adjusts the rate of the heartbeat to the carbonic acid content of the blood. If the muscle stops working and the carbonic acid content of the blood becomes lower, the action of the heart becomes slower.

We have to remember that the action of the heart is related to the needs of the body as a whole. Mental excitement stimulates a nerve which makes the heartbeat faster. When we are depressed or frightened, a different nerve is stimulated which makes the heartbeat slower."

How do we take in Oxygen ?

Anjana asked - "Ma'am, we can't live without oxygen. But how do we take in oxygen?"

Ma'am replied - "We have special groups of cells which enable us to take in oxygen. These cells are in the lungs. We breathe in oxygen through the lungs and from the lungs, the oxygen passes into the bloodstream and is carried to all parts of the body. The breathing process supplies the cells with oxygen for respiration.

The oxygen that the blood carries is part of the air we breathe. Air is usually taken in through the nose and is warmed and cleaned on its way to the throat. From the throat air goes through the voice box, into the windpipe and then to the lungs.

The windpipe splits into two tubes in the chest. These tubes are called the bronchial tubes and each tube leads to one of the body's two lungs. Here the tube begins to branch into smaller and smaller tubes. Each of the tiniest tubes opens into a cluster of thin-walled air sacs, bunched like grapes and covered with a fine net of capillaries.

From the heart, the waste-carrying blood is pumped into the capillaries of the air sacs. And here, a quick change takes place. The waste gas—carbon dioxide passes through the thin capillary walls into the air sacs. Oxygen from the air sacs passes into the capillaries and the red blood cells. Now the blood has oxygen and it moves to the left side of the heart. And from there, the heart pumps the blood with the oxygen to all the cells of the body."

How do Antibiotics work ?

Sanjeev asked - "Ma'am, how do antibiotics work ?"

Ma'am replied - "Antibiotics are chemicals. These chemicals are put into our body to kill or stop the growth of certain kinds of germs. They help us to fight diseases.

The word antibiotics comes from two Greek words meaning "against life". Antibiotics work against the forms of life that we call germs. It was in 1942, that the name "antibiotics" was first applied to these medicines.

Many antibiotics are made from microbes. What are microbes ? Microbes are tiny living things. Bacteria and moulds are microbes. Microbes constantly fight for survival. And in the course of the struggle, they produce complex chemicals in their bodies. By investigating the chemical products of microbes, scientists have discovered many chemicals that kill disease germs. So they were used to make antibiotics.

How do antibiotics work ? When they are put into the body, they cut off the germ's supply of oxygen. Without oxygen, germs can't go on dividing. There are antibiotics which prevent germs from taking in food from the patient's body. So the germ starves to death. Sometimes the germ mistakes the antibiotics for part of its usual diet. The germ "eats" the antibiotic and gets poisoned. There are some antibiotics which kill the germs instantly, and there are some which weaken the germs and let the body's natural

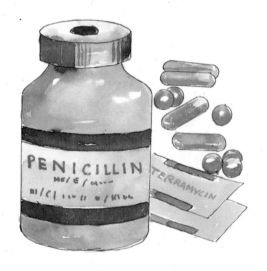

defences take over."

What is Endocrinology ?

Jhumna asked - "Ma'am, what is endocrinology ?"

Ma'am explained - "In our body, there are certain organs which produce chemical substances that keep the body fit. These chemical substances are called hormones. The group of organs which produce these hormones is called the endocrine system. Endocrinology is the study of these organs and hormones.

The endocrine glands are : the pituitary, the thyroid, the parathyroids, the pineal, the adrenals, the testes, the ovaries, part of the pancreas, the sex glands and the thymus. They are called "glands of internal secretion" because they send their substances directly into the blood. stream to be distributed throughout the body. Some of these produce many hormones while some produce only one.

They regulate many functions of the body : the size of your body, the rate of growth, your weight, your hair, and even the masculine and feminine aspect of you. Moreover, they regulate your body temperature, the amount of urine produced, the rate of metabolism, the calcium and sugar levels in the blood, the transformation of proteins into energy giving substances.

The hormones especially affect the reproductive system. They also determine, to a certain extent, the personality of the individual. Your mental and physical alertness is also determined by the hormones.

Even the experts on the subject are not being able to understand how these organs are able to do all this."

What is the Pituitary gland ?

Raka asked - "Ma'am, what is the pituitary gland ?"

Ma'am replied - "The pituitary gland is part of the endocrine system of the body. It is the most important part of the body in regulating growth, the production of milk

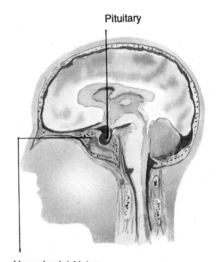

Pituitary

Hypophysial Veins

and in controlling all other endocrine glands.

Do you know how big is our pituitary gland ? It is about the size of a pea and it also weighs about the same. It is joined to the under surface of the brain and is protected by a bony structure.

It is further divided into two parts called "lobes"-the anterior lobe and the posterior lobe. Into this posterier lobe, go more than 50,000 nerve fibres connecting it with various parts of the body !

The hormones, which the pituitary gland produce, affect the metabolism of the body which has to do with the transforming of food into various forms of energy. This gland controls growth in children by acting on another gland, the thyroid. It also controls the sexual development of the person. Moreover it is involved with certain muscles, the kidneys and other organs.

Tumours that may grow on this gland can make it overactive or underactive. One result of this activity can be to make people grow to giants or develop so poorly that they will be the size of dwarfs."

What is the Pineal gland ?

Shubho asked - "Ma'am, is the pineal gland a part of the endocrine system ?"

Ma'am replied - "Yes, that's right. It is one of the glands of the endocrine system. These glands are also called "ductless glands" because the hormones they produce do not go into the ducts or tubes. Rather they are absorbed directly into the blood stream.

The pineal gland is a mysterious little organ. It is about the size of a small pill and is located in the central part of the brain towards the top of the head. The physicians in ancient times thought the gland to be responsible for our thinking. But the physicians of today believe that this gland produces some internal secretion which is being absorbed by the blood stream. Moreover it affects the other endocrine glands in the work they do. Since it is quite close to the pituitary gland, it possibly has some effect on that gland."

What does the Liver do ?

Megha asked - "Ma'am, what does the liver do ? Is it the largest gland of the body ?"

Ma'am replied - "Yes, it is. And next to the brain, it is the heaviest organ. The average human liver weighs about one kilogram.

It is large because of it's work. It not only manufactures digestive juices known as bile but it is also a filter in which all the food received from the intestine (except fat)

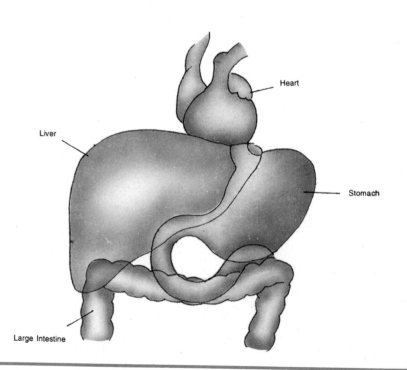

Heart

Liver

Stomach

Large Intestine

goes through a chemical process. It is like a blood-filled sponge which absorbs the food digested in the intestine.

What happens to food in the liver ? It is "reconstructed". That is foreign protein is rebuilt to form human protein. The liver also "detoxifies" food. When the body takes in nicotine and coffeine, the liver transforms these "poisons" into harmless compounds. Liver cells also destroy becilli that may enter our body.

The liver is located between the heart and the intestine. Therefore it acts as a kind of dam for the liquids we take in. If you drink a large quantity of liquid, the liver swells up."

How do our Kidneys function ?

Sweta asked - "Ma'am, our kidneys lie on each side of the spine near the waistline and are about ten centimetres long, are not they ?"

Ma'am replied - "That's right. The kidneys are two, flat, bean-shaped solid organs which help the body by removing unwanted substances. They also regulate the amount of water and other substances in the blood.

In the outer part of each kidney, capillaries form tiny loops that make up a ball-like shape covered by a delicate membrane. In each kidney there are about 1,500,000 of these tiny balls called "Glomeruli". More blood flows through the kidneys every minute than through any other organ. The Glomeruli allow some of the fluid of the blood which carries the finest dissolved materials to pass through the membranes.

The fluid that passes through is "urine" which is collected within a cuplike wall which covers each glomerulus. A very delicate tube, called a "tubule", drains the urine from the cups.

As the urine flows through the tiny tubules, the lining cells are busy exchanging materials between the blood and urine. Substances that the body needs are taken back into the blood. Much of the water in the tubules also return to the blood. In this way, the kidneys help to keep the body properly moist. The kidney tubules also help to regulate the acid level in the blood.

All the small tubules collect in the inner part of each kidney and open into delicate sac, the pelvis of the kidney. The urine then goes down two tubes called "ureters", that connect the kidneys to the bladder.

Without kidneys, we would not be able to survive."

Renal Capsule
Arcuate Artery
Renal Artery
Renal Vein
Renal Pelvis
Calyx
Ureter
Urine
Pyramid
Medulla
Cortex

Why do Fleas live on dogs and cats?

Are Jellyfish really fishes?

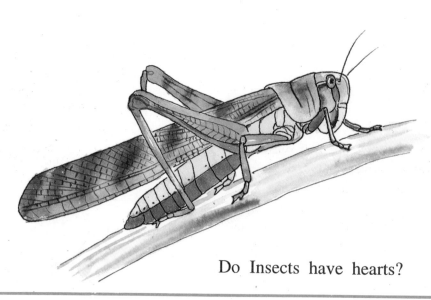

Do Insects have hearts?

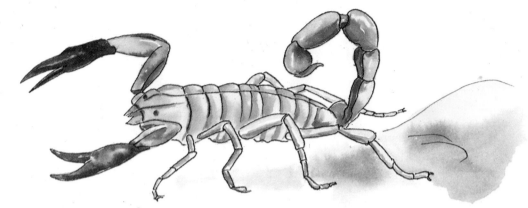

How dangerous is a Scorpion?

Animal Life

Do the Houseflies eat solid food?

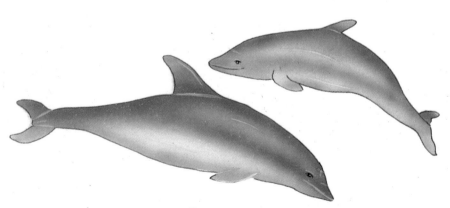

Is Dolphin a fish?

Do Insects have hearts ?

Ranjani was very excited as she asked - "Ma'am, my brother was saying that insects have heart ! Such tiny ones. Do they really have hearts ?"

Ma'am replied - "Yes, ofcourse. If you look carefully at a mosquito larva, or some cater- pillars, you will see a long tube running along the top of the body, right under the skin. The insect's heart is part of this tube, which opens just under the brain. There are tiny openings with valves along this tube like heart. Blood is sucked into the heart through these openings. The heart contracts and forces blood to flow toward the head. In the head, the blood pours out over the brain and then flows backward through the body. And as it flows backward, it bathes the body organs, muscles and nervous system. It brings digested food and takes away waste material.

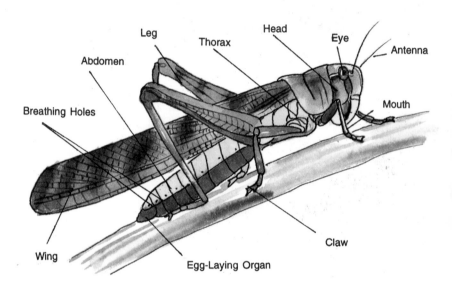

But an insects blood is not red like our's. It doesn't carry oxygen and so it has no hamoglobin which makes blood red. An insect has nerves and brain too. A large nerve center in the head is the insects brain. The brain receives sensations and sends messages to certain muscles to make them work. But this is done automatically.

Did you know that a grasshopper has about 900 muscles? That is the reason why the insects are remarkably strong. They have too many muscles and the muscles are very thick."

Which Insect has the longest life ?

Sanjeev asked - "Ma'am, the insects have a short life span compared to other living things on earth. Which insect has the longest life ?"

Ma'am replied - "There is a species of the cicada that lives for 17 years. There are more than 800 species or kinds of cicadas and 100 of these are found in North America. But the 17 year old cicada is found only in USA. Most species of cicadas live only for two years.

A very interesting thing about the 17 year life span of cicada is that it sleeps in the ground for those entire 17 years, comes out to enjoy only five weeks of life in the sun and then dies ! When the young are hatched from eggs, they drop down, burrow into the ground and attach themselves to roots. And these young cicadas which are called "nymphs", remain there motionless for 17 years, sucking the sap of the roots.

And then they climb the trunk of a tree, into the light, their skins split open and the mature cicada emerges. It lives for five weeks in the sun and then dies. Though it has the longest life, it spends almost all of it in sleep!"

How dangerous is a Scorpion ?

Rekha asked - "Ma'am, is a scorpion dangerous ? It looks quite dangerous with its strong pincers."

Ma'am replied - "Scorpions have caused deaths several times. In Mexico, there is the Durango scorpion the bite of which can kill a person within an hour and over a period of 35 years, it has caused the deaths of about 1,600 people.

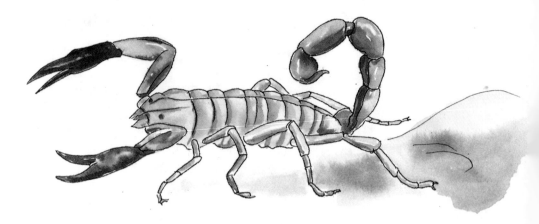

Scorpions are found mainly in warm climates. There are about 500 species of scorpions all over the world. Scorpions vary in size from one centimetre to about 17 centimetres. The largest are found in the tropics.

Scorpions are mainly active at night. During the day, they hid in dark places such as beneath a stone, in bark, in the dark corners of buildings. Adult scorpions always live and travel alone. Young scorpions are born alive and cling to the mother's back. She does not feed them and after several days, they go off on their own.

Scorpions, related to the spiders, when walks, carries its tail arched over its body. When it grasps its prey in its pincers, it bends its stinger over its head and plunges it into the victim. The poison kills or paralyses its prey."

Why do Fleas live on dogs and cats ?

Danny said - "Ma'am, I have got a dog and a cat in my house. Fleas keep on troubling them. Can't the fleas leave them alone ?"

Ma'am replied - "The flea lives on dogs and cats by sucking their blood. Fleas also infest rats, rabbits, squirrels, birds and nearly all other warm blooded animals. Even on human beings. During the middle ages, flea-infested rat spread bubonic plague throughout Europe. The flea lived on the diseased rat until the rat died. And then the flea jumped upon a human being, carrying with it the disease germs.

There are actually hundreds of species of fleas. They are parasites. A parasite is a plant or animal that lives with, in or on another living organism. A flea has a small round head and mouth parts that are adapted to sucking. It has a tiny body, no wings and three pairs of legs.

Did you know a flea is a wonderful jumper? It is, infact, the champion jumper of all creatures. With the help of its long hind legs, it can jump 18 to 20 centimetres into the air and can jump forward atleast 30 centimetres!"

Why is the Fruit fly so useful to science?

Rebecca asked - "Ma'am, why is the fruit fly such an important insect to science ?"

Ma'am replied - "The fruit fly which is known as "drosophila" is one of the most useful insects known to science because it is used in the study of heredity, which means the passing on of characteristics from parents to offspring. To study 30 human generations, we would take 500 years or more. But by using the fruit fly, we can study 30 generations in a single year. In a few hours, a number of female fruit flies can lay enough eggs to produce a thousand new adults, all emerging on the same day. They lay their eggs only in fruit that has begun to rot or decay. When the young are born, they feed on the fermentation which the decaying fruit produces.

The fruit flies can be studied with the naked eye and surgical operations can be performed on them under a microscope. Most of our present knowledge of heredity has been gained from the study of fruit flies!

There are actually two different kinds of fruit flies. The drosophila which is harmless. And the Mediterranean fruit fly, which looks somewhat like a housefly with orange and black markings. The Mediterrnean fruit fly is one of the most destructive pests."

What is the secret of a Fire fly's light ?

Shubho asked - " Once I saw a whole bunch of fireflies moving about at night. They looked so very beautiful ! Ma'am, where does it get its light from ?"

Ma'am replied - "The light of the firefly is very much like other kinds of light except that it is producd without heat ! This kind of light is called "luminescence". Fireflies have luciferin and luciferase in their bodies. The luciferase enables the luciferin to burn up and produce lights.

You will be surprised that even the scientists are still mystified because there are many things about the fireflies light which cann't be explained ! The scientists can produce the same kind of light in the laboratory but for that, they have to take the ingredients from the firefly ! Chemists can't produce it synthetically. It remains one of the secrets of nature.

One of you might grow up to be a scientist and then you would tell us how do these little creatures flash on and off."

Do the Houseflies eat solid food ?

Rehana asked - "Ma'am I have seen houseflies on solid food which means they do eat solid food, don't they ?

Ma'am replied - " No, I am afraid they do not. Houseflies can not eat solid food

because they have no equipment for biting. The mouth parts of the fly are made for sucking up liquid food. When a fly lands on solid food, it spreads saliva on it which makes it liquid. What looks like the fly's "tongue" is really a snout like the elephant's trunk. It has two lobes at the end which act as funnels for drawing in its liquid food.

People think that house flies bite them. But its not true. Other types of flies like sand flies or stable flies, which are blood sucking by nature, are the ones which bite people.

You may be wondering that if the housefly does not bite, why is it considered so dangerous ? It is dangerous because of the sticky glue which covers its tongue and because of the bristling hairs which cover its claws, padded feet and body. Due to these, dust and dirt cling to the fly, which may be full of the bacteria of various diseases. And then if the fly touches the food we eat, these diseased bacteria enter our body".

How are some Insects harmful to us ?

Megha said - "Ma'am, bees give us honey and so many insect's carry pollen from one flower to the other, making the flowers bloom. Insects are so very helpful, aren't they?"

Ma'am replied - "Yes, they are very helpful. But there are some insects which are harmful to us. They sting bite or carry diseases.

Some kinds of mosquitoes carry germs that cause diseases, such as yellow fever, malaria and sleeping sickness. The germs that cause the disease are picked up by the mosquito and then passed on to another person it bites.

Flies spread diseases such as cholera, dysentry, hepatitis and typhoid. These diseases, like all those that are spread or carried by insects, are less opt to occur if an area is kept free of dirt and if the insects are prevented from breeding.

Black widow spiders which are found from Southern California to Chile usually in damp spots are extremely harmful. Its poison causes great pain and stiffening of the muscles of the abdomen. Many victims of the black widow spider die.

These are some of the insects that are harmful to us."

Where do Bacteria live ?

Rohan asked - "Ma'am, where do bacteria live ?"

Ma'am replied - "There are at least two thousand species of bacteria and they live practically everywhere and anywhere. Some live in the mouths, noses and intestines of animals including us. Others live on fallen leaves, dead trees, animal wastes, carcasses.

They live in fresh and salt water, in milk and in most foods. They live in dust, soil and sewage. Some bacteria are able to use as food such substances as hydrogen gas, ammonia, iron compounds and paraffin. A few feed on acid and gases that are not ordinarily kill bacteria. And bacteria can remain inactive for long periods of time. You will be surprised to know that bacteria have been found frozen in salt deposits that are hundreds of millions of years old! These bacteria have become active in the laboratory."

How are Bacteria useful to us ?

Ajanta asked - "Ma'am, whenever we say bacteria we think of germs that are harmful and cause diseases. But there are bacteria which are useful to us, aren't they ?"

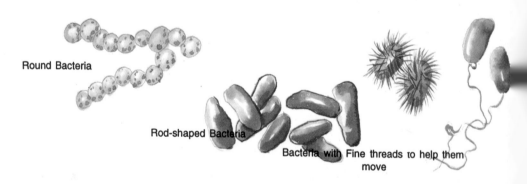

Round Bacteria

Rod-shaped Bacteria

Bacteria with Fine threads to help them move

poisonous to us.

Bacteria are the most common form of life on earth and they can be seen only through microscope. A bacteria consists of only one cell and they have some features of both plants and animals.

Most bacteria are killed by extreme heat but some bacteria live in hot springs. Freezing may check their growth but does Ma'am replied - "Yes , they are. There are over two thousand different kinds of bacteria and most of them are either harmless or helpful to us.

Bacteria help us in digesting our food. In our intestine, there are a great many bacteria. As the bacteria eat, they break down food. At the same time, they make certain vitamins which the body then uses

Moreover, bacteria help to keep the earth free of dead matter . Its due to the bacteria that the dead plants and animals decay. While eating, the bacteria break down the complicated substances in these organisms into simpler ones. Which are then restored to the soil, water and air in forms that can be used by living plants and animals.

Bacteria are also a vital link in the food chain that supports life. Some bacteria called nitrogen-fixing bacteria, live in the soil and help change nitrogen into substances that plants can use. We depend on such plants for food.

We are fond of cheese. Do you know how is it made ? Cheese, vinegar are made by the fermentation process which is caused by bacteria. The same fermentation is also used in industry to make substances essential for paints, plastics, cosmetics, candy and several other products. It is also used to make certain drugs.

These are only a few ways, there are still many more ways they are used everyday."

What is the difference between Bacteria and Viruses ?

Rohan asked - "Ma'am, people usually think bacteria and viruses in terms of diseases. But are not they quite different from each other ?"

Ma'am replied - "Yes, they are. There are at least two thousand species of bacteria most of which are either harmless or helpful.

Both viruses and bacteria are very small. A bacteria consists of only one cell. A single drop of sour milk may contain 100,000,000 bacteria! Viruses are so small that they can only be seen through an electronic microscope.

Viruses grow and multiply only when they are inside living cells. Outside living cells, they do not change in any way and seem lifeless. They can't grow unless they are inside the cells of animals, plants or bacteria. Viruses that attack man and animals are called animal viruses. Those that attack plants are called plant viruses. And those that attack bacteria are called bacterial viruses.

The viruses which infect us may be breathed in or swallowed or they may enter through an opening in the skin. Some of them destroy cells simply by growing in them. Others cause the membranes separating two cells to dissolve and still others cause cells to become malignant."

How does an Amoeba eat ?

Dheeraj said - "Ma'am, an amoeba is also very small and can be seen only under a microscope. I did not know it's also considered an animal !"

Ma'am replied - "When we think of animal, we generally think of large creatures moving about on earth. But an animal can have only one cell also. Amoeba, the jelly like creature is one-celled. The common species of amoeba lives in freshwater streams and ponds while other amoebas live on the bottom of fresh and salt water bodies and in damp soils and foods.

Do you know how does an amoeba eat ? It's very interesting. If you see an amoeba, you will notice that it constantly changes its shape. It moves by pushing out one side and then another. As some of the jellylike substance is pushed out, it forms what are called false feet or "pseudopodia". When the pseudopodia reach food, they wrap themselves around it and take it into the main body. An amoeba does not have mouth. This is the way it eats.

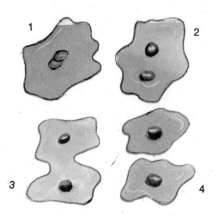

The amoeba belongs to the protozoa, which is the lowest division of the animal kingdom. It has no lungs or gills. But it absorbs oxygen from the water, gives off carbon dioxide and digests its food as other animals do.

If you touch an amoeba, it will roll itself into a tiny ball. It also avoids bright light and water which is too hot or too cold.

Another interesting thing about an amoeba is that in a full-sized amoeba, the nucleus, a tiny dot in the center of the protoplasm, divides into two parts. After this, the amoeba itself divides, forming into new individual animals. When these become full grown, each of them divide again."

Are Jellyfish really fishes ?

Radhika asked - "Ma'am, jellyfish are made of jelly, aren't they ?"
Ma'am replied - "Yes, they are almost entirely made of jelly. Did you know jelly fish are actually not fishes ?" Fishes are vertebrates. That is fishes have backbones. But jellyfish do not have backbones. Their bodies are bags of jelly with a hollow inside. They are shaped like an overturned bowl. The bowl of the jellyfish is made up of two thin layers of tissue with jelly like material between them. If a jellyfish is removed from the water, it dries up very quickly because 98% of its body is water.

The jellyfish has tentacles, hanging

from the edge of the bowl, which gather food and are sometimes used for swimming. Some of these tentacles are barbed and pierce the body of the prey. These barbed cells are connected to poison glands. The jellyfish protect themselves with a sting that can sometimes be dangerous. If the jellyfish is quite small, being stung by one may not be too dangerous. But when it comes to the big ones, it may be dangerous. There are big ones with a bowl of nearly 4 metres in diameter and with tentacles more than 30 metres long ! If it embraces us, we might even become paralysed. The Portuguese man - of - war which is one of the largest jellyfish, can kill and eat a full-sized mackerel. It can cause serious injury to human beings. There is a kind of jellyfish found off the coast of Australia called "the sea wasp" which has been known to cause death in many cases."

Do Eels ever travel on land ?

John asked - "Ma'am, eels look like water snakes, don't they ?"

Ma'am replied - "Yes, they do. But actually they are fishes. Like all other fishes they have backbones, they live in water and breathe through gills. They are cold blooded which means their body temperature varies with the surrounding temperature.

Most eels live in the sea. All eels shed their eggs in salt water. You will be surprised to know that some eels travel on land to go to the salt water to spawn. Fresh water eels have to travel over land to reach salt water!

How do they survive on land ? It's their body mucus which helps them breathe through their skins and also keeps their bodies from drying out. You may not see eels on land because they travel at night. But you may find some eels in wells or ponds that are far away from moving water.

The eels far inland are females. The male eels are smaller than the females, usually no more than 0.3 to 0.5 metres long. They are found closer to the sea in slightly salt water."

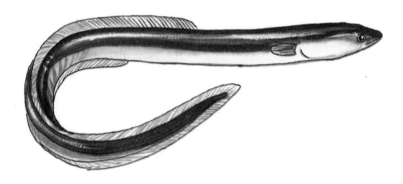

Are Eels dangerous ?

Damini asked - "Ma'am, are eels dangerous ?"

Ma'am replied - "Moray eels are the ones considered by many people to be dangerous. They live among rocks and in coral reefs where they hide in holes and crannies. When they are hungry, they dart out and snap up prey that swims too near. Their jaws are very powerful and they have sharp teeth.

The ancient Romans considered the moray eels bite poisonous but people who have been bitten by moray eels have shown no poisonous effects. The morays can, however, attack a human being under certain conditions and give a person quite a savage bite.

There is another kind of eels which are known as conger eels. Some of these eels grow to giant size. A conger eel has been caught weighing 72 kilos and 2.7 metres long ! Moray eels may grow up to 3 metres though most of them are 1 metre long.

An electric eel is not an eel! It belongs to the same order of fish as carp, catfish!"

Is Sponge an animal ?

Nishi said - "Ma'am, I was so surprised when I came to know that a sponge is an animal! It looks like a plant, doesn't it ?"

Ma'am replied - "Yes, it does. Sponges are among the strangest members of the animal kingdom. There are more than five thousand different kinds of sponges. They are of different colours like green brown yellow, red, orange and white. They may be shaped like fans, domes, vases, bowls or trumpets.

If you touch a sponge, it does not react. It does not have a head or mouth. It has no eyes, ears, feelers or other sense organs. It has no heart, stomach, muscles or nervous system. If a living sponge is cut into two, all you see is a slimy mass with holes or channels running through it.

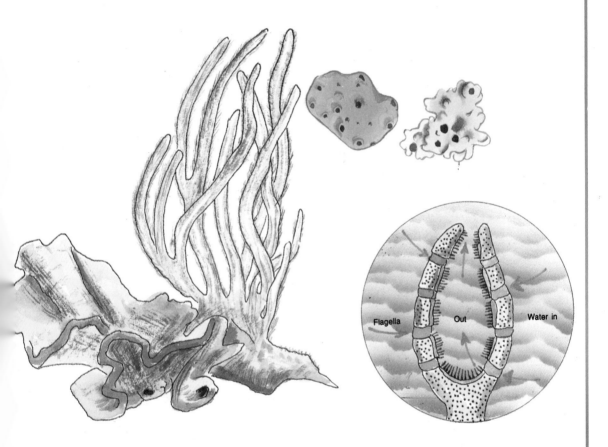

Flagella   Out   Water in

What makes a sponge an animal ? The way it feeds. A sponge captures its food like an animal. It does not make its own food like a green plant does. It captures tiny plants and animals from the water around it. The tube wall of a sponge is like a sieve or fitter that strains tiny plants and animals out of the water. This makes sponge an animal."

Why isn't a Whale considered a fish ?

Namit said - "A whale has a fish-shaped body and lives in water. But still, it is not considered a fish. Why is it so ma'am ?"

Ma'am replied - "A whale is a mammal. That is the baby whale is fed on its mother's milk like other mammals. While a fish is hatched from the egg, a baby whale is born alive and for sometime, it stays close to the mother who takes very good care of it. Moreover whales breathe differently from fish. Instead of gills, they have lungs and they take in air through two nostrils or "blow holes" on the top of their heads. When they go under-water, these nostrils are closed by little valves so that no water can get in.

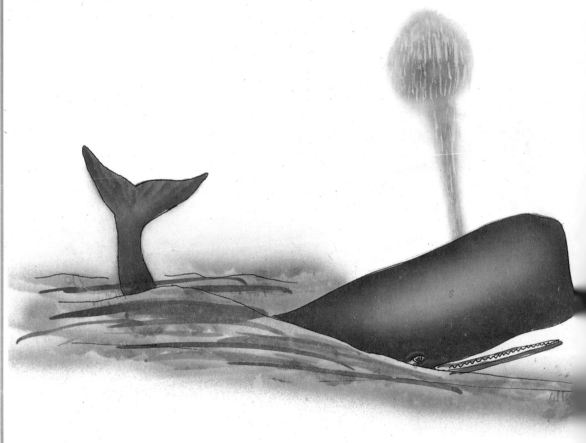

We can say that the whale is a water mammal and is descended from ancestors that lived on land. During the thousands and thousands of years, they have been living in water. Therefore they have grown to resemble fish in their shape and other outside features. But they are built and they live like land animals. For instance, a whale's flippers have the bones of a five-fingered hand. Some whales even have the bones of hind legs in their flesh !"

How many kinds of Whales are there ?

Suruchi asked - "How many kinds of whales are there ?"

Ma'am replied - "The scientists generally divide whales into two groups : odontoceti and mysticeti. Odontoceti means "whales with teeth". Mysticeti means "moustached whales". These whales have "moustaches" of baleen or whalebone, hanging from the roof of the mouth. Baleen is a fibrous, horny substance, fringed along the inner edges. Using their baleen, these whales strain huge quantities of small food out of the water.

The baleen whales are the largest animals ever to live on earth. They are even bigger than dinosaurs. The blue whale which is the largest of this type, may be 30 metres long and weigh more than 110 tonnes !

There are three families of baleen whales : the right whales, the fin whales and the grey whales. Blue whales are the largest species of fin whales. These whales are found in seas the world over.

Baleen whales differ in so many ways from toothed whales that they are believed to be only very distantly related."

How many kinds of Sharks are there ?

Suchit asked - "Ma'am, how many kinds of sharks are there ? Are they dangerous ?"

Ma'am replied - "There are more than 150 different kinds of sharks. Some of them are dangerous, but all are not. The most dreaded of all fish is the great white shark which is sometimes 12 metres long. It definitely attacks human beings.

The sharks that often follow ships are harmless creatures, hoping to pick up food from the ships. Even small fishes are not afraid of them. This is also true of some very big sharks, that is, unless they are attacked. One of these is the whale shark. This shark is found near the cape of Good Hope and in the Mediterranean, Pacific and Caribbean right up to Florida. It may be over 11 metres long and weigh more than 13 tonnes.

The other "safe" big shark is the basking shark. It is the biggest fish of the North Atlantic and is over 13 metres long. It likes to bask in the sun with its back partly out of the water.

They all live in salt water except for one species. In central America, there is a Lake called Nicaragua where lives a fresh water shark."

Is Dolphin a fish ?

Anupama asked - "Ma'am, is dolphin a fish ?"

Ma'am explained - "No, it is not. Dolphins are small whales, ranging in length from about 1 to 3.5 metres. They are called "dolphins" or "porpoises".

Whales, dolphins, porpoises all belong to the same family of aquatic mammals called "CETACEAN". Dolphins are small whales that belong to the toothed - whale group. Porpoises are a kind of dolphin without beaks with a triangular back fin and spade-shaped teeth.

Dolphins live on cuttlefish, squids, crabs and many kinds of fish which they chase and capture. The gramphs, or killer whale, which is really a large dolphin, is the only one in this group that eats other warm-blooded animals. It is about 9 metres long and it easily catches seals. The other dolphins are not often more than 3 metres long and their heads are quite small.

Dolphins seem to enjoy following ships. And they live in great herds. The common dolphin which may be found in all temperate and tropical seas, has a tail, shaped like a moon."

Why are Dolphins considered intelligent ?

Sashank asked - "Ma'am, dolphins are considered very intelligent, aren't they ?"

Ma'am replied - "Yes, they are unusually intelligent animals. Many of them have even imitated human speech quite distinctly.

Scientists are extremely interested in

the call notes the dolphins use in communicating to each other and in the way dolphins move through the water avoiding danger. It is believed that they are capable of making sounds that have more "meaning" than any other creature in the sea.

Dolphins can also solve problems. If a piece of food is stuck under a rock, they can find a way to "blow" the food out from under the rock.

The students who study animal behaviour consider dolphins intelligent because they are able to invent and play games. If there is a feather floating about in a tank of water, a dolphin will get it and bring it near the jet of water entering the tank. The feather drifts into the jet and goes shooting off. The dolphin pursues it, catches it, brings it back and again releases it into the jet ! This is a sure sign of intelligence."

Which Whale has got a long Ivory tusk ?

Rahul said - "Ma'am, I have seen pictures of whales which have got ivory tusks which looks like swords."

Ma'am replied - "These whales are called Narwhal. A narwhal is a type of whale, one of the most interesting and fascinating creature. It is found chiefly in Arctic water and has something that can't be found on any other whale : a long ivory tusk. It is the male narwhal which has this long ivory tusk on the left side of its mouth. This tusk sticks out in front like a sword !

The narwhal is one of the toothed whales. Toothed whales generally live on various types of fish that they chase and capture. Sperm whales are the largest of the toothed whales. They may be twenty metres long and their heads are huge. Another toothed whale is the bottle-nosed whale which has strange bony crests on either side of its head."

Where do Penguins lay their eggs ?

Sanjeev asked - "Ma'am penguins live in the Antarctic, most of which is covered with snow and ice. Where do these birds lay their eggs ?"

Ma'am replied - "That's a very interesting question. During the Antarctic winter, February to October, the penguins live in the sea. In October, which is early spring there, they come out of the sea and start a long trek to the breeding grounds, which is the rocky Antarctic coast.

To reach there, they have to walk, slide, scramble and toboggan 100 kilometres across the sea ice. Its the males who usually arrive first. They go directly to their nests of previous year. The nests are made of stones.

The male and the female make a nest together before the eggs are laid. They collect stones, carry the stones in their beaks. They collect and guard the stones in turn. The stones are dropped by one partner while the other arranges them into a neat pile.

In mid-November, the female penguin lays two bluish-white eggs which are being hatched by both male and female by turns. When one is hatching, the other goes to the sea to eat. And its always the female who returns just as the chicks are coming out of the eggs. Till four weeks, they take turns in guarding the chicks and feeding themselves. And then the little ones are ready to go to the sea with their parents."

Why do people hunt Walruses ?

Nidhi asked - "Ma'am, why do people hunt walruses ?"

Ma'am replied - "Eskimos and other

Arctic people have depended on the walrus to supply them with food, fuel, clothing and equipment. Practically every part of the body is used. The blubber supplies oil for fuel. For clothing, the leathery hides are used. The flesh is used for food. And the ivory tusks are used to make many different kinds of objects. Eskimos have used these tusks to carve small decorative objects.

The walrus may vanish if steps are not taken to protect it. The total walrus population is down to only 40,000 to 50,000.

A walrus is a huge mammal that lives in Arctic waters off both coasts of northern North America and also off north eastern Siberia. It measures from 2.5 to 3.5 metres in length when full grown and weighs upto 1,400 kilograms. They have a thick hide which is tough and wrinkled and which has almost no fur. They grow tusks to be used in digging for molluscs and for fighting.

They live together in herds. They stay in far northern waters during the summer. In the fall, they drift southward with the ice and in the spring, they swim northward again."

Why are Otters called the "old men of the sea" ?

Mayankh asked - "Ma'am, why are otters called the "old men of the sea" ?

Ma'am replied - "The sea otters have white whiskers from which they get the nickname the "old men of the sea". Their thick fur is dark brown and has a frosted appearance. The sea otter is found off the western coast of North America, from California to Alaska and in other northern waters.

Sea otters are larger and heavier than fresh-water otters. The fresh water otter is found in streams and lakes from Mexico to Alaska. Its coat is rich dark brown. This otter is always on the move. Its home is usually a hole dug into the bank of a stream or lake. The hole leads to a den lined with leaves. Here the young ones are born in late winter or early spring. Before they can swim, the mother carries them about on her back in the water.

Otters love water. And both the kinds of otters are found in North America. Otters belong to a group of animals call the "mustelids" which comes from the Latin and means "weasel". Other members of this family include weasels, skunks and badgers."

What are Pinnipeds ?

Tarini asked - "What are pinnipeds ?"

Ma'am replied - "Pinnipeds are fin-footed mammals with limbs that they use as paddles or flippers. Walrus, sea-lion, seal and sea elephants are different kinds of pinnipeds. They all are flesh-eaters. They live in water and are expert divers. They can go from sixty to ninety metres down in search of food to eat. Their bodies are tapered and streamlined with a thick layer of blubber which also serves as a reserve of food when needed.

There are about thirty different kinds of pinnipeds which live in the world's ocean. Most of them live in the cold waters of the Arctic and Antarctic ocean and in the nearby areas of the Atlantic and the Pacific. A few kinds range into warmer waters and several forms live in fresh water lakes.

When they are under water, their nostrils close. Many of them have big eyes that are useful for seeing in the dim depths.

Most of them have sharp backward pointing teeth so that they can seize prey and direct it down the throat.

They live together in large herds."

What is a Sea Elephant ?

Aditya asked - "Ma'am, what is a sea elephant ?"

Ma'am replied - "A sea elephant is a giant seal. There are two species of the sea elephant: One, the Southern elephant seal which lives in waters around Antarctica.

The other, the northern elephant seal, lives in waters off the coast of lower California and breeds in Guadaloupe and other small islands.

Both species look very much alike and grow to about the same size. Big adult males may measure nearly six metres long and weigh over 3,000 kilos. The females are much smaller, usually not more than two or three metres long. When a sea elephant is born, it weighs forty to forty-five kilo.

The male elephant seal has a long, dangling snout. A male inflates his snout and roars loudly when there is any kind of danger.

They almost vanished for they were hunted for their hides and oil. The Mexican government stepped in and protected them."

Why did Dinosaurs become extinct ?

Shabnam asked - "Ma'am, why did dinosaurs become extinct ?"

Ma'am replied - "Dinosaurs developed in many different ways but none of them ever developed a good brain. One reason dinosaurs disappeared may be that they were just not able to survive and escape from all their natural enemies.

Many scientists believe that changes in the earth and in climate killed off the dinosaurs. Swamps dried up, mountains appeared, and certain dinosaurs could not live on dry land. Changes in climate produced changes in vegetation and since many dinosaurs were plant eaters, their food supply disappeared. And as the earth began to have seasons, shifting from hot summers to snowy winters, dinosaurs could not fit themselves to the changes and gradually died out.

The first dinosaurs were no bigger than

a turkey, and like a turkey, they walked on their hind legs. In time, they grew so heavier and longer that their legs would not support them on land. So they had to spend most of their lives in rivers and swamps where water could keep their huge bodies afloat."

How do we know what Dinosaurs were like ?

Rahil asked - "Ma'am, about 60 million years ago, the dinosaurs died out because changing conditions made life impossible for them. Then how do we know what they were like ?"

Ma'am replied - "Everything we know about dinosaurs comes from fossils. These are remains which these creatures left in the earth.

Scientists believe that dinosaurs first appeared on the earth about 180 million years ago and died out about 60 million years ago. The most common fossils are petrified remains of what were the hard parts of their bodies - bones, teeth and claws. Scientists study these remains and from them reconstruct how the whole body of the dinosaur was built.

Petrified tendons and skin provide more clues. Fossils can also be footprints that were made in wet sand or mud that hardened into stone over the ages. From these, it is possible to tell how the dinosaurs walked and whether it was on two legs or four. The rarest fossils of all are the dinosaur eggs.

In this way we can tell that the Brontosaurus, one of the family of dinosaurs was 20 to 25 metres long and weighed about 38 tonnes. It lived in swamps and was a plant eater. A dinosaur called

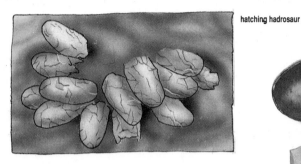

hatching hadrosaur

This is a cast made of a nest of *Protoceratops* eggs. The nest must have been covered in soft sand and mud shortly after the eggs were laid.

The external skeleton of this trilobite contained a hard mineral called calcite that does not decay easily. Parts of animals containing calcite are often found as fossils.

Allosaurus had sharp teeth and it fed upon Brontosaurus. The scientists have found fossil teeth of the Allosaurus among the broken and deeply scratched bones of Brontosaurus !"

When did we first find out about Dinosaurs ?

Sweta asked - "Ma'am, when did we first find out about dinosaurs ?"

Ma'am replied - "There is doubt as to when we first found out dinosaur's bones. Footprints have been known for many years. A dinosaur skeleton may have been seen at Haddonfield, New jersey toward the end of 1700's.

The bones that are still available for examination and identification were discovered in England. One set was found in 1822 and is now in the British Museum of Natural History in London.

Dinosaurs specimens have been found in great numbers in the USA, Canada, India, Africa, Brazil, Argentina, Australia, Mangolia, China, France, Germany, Portugal and Russia. Dinosaurs died out everywhere about 65,000,000 years ago. And the first kind of human being appeared less than 2,500,000 years ago. By the time, human being appeared, dinosaurs were already extinct."